DRAWN AWAY

OTHER BOOKS BY JAY R. LEACH

How Should We Then Live

Behold The Man

The Blood Runs Through It

DRAWN AWAY

COUNTERING AN UNGODLY SPIRITUALITY

Through an Authentic Godly Spirituality
In a Skeptical Relativistic Age

JAY R. LEACH

Pastor, Author, and Teacher

ISBN: 978-1-4669-5609-4 (sc)
ISBN: 978-1-4669-5608-7 (e)

Library of Congress Control Number: 2012916946

Trafford rev. 10/12/2012

 www.trafford.com

North America & international
toll-free: 1 888 232 4444 (USA & Canada)
phone: 250 383 6864 ♦ fax: 812 355 4082

CONTENTS

I dedicate this book to our Lord and Savior,
Jesus Christ and for His service.
I trust it will be used in His hands as another instrument
to help prepare the Bride for His soon return.
And to those whom He has brought into my life,
who exemplify true godly spirituality.

I want to thank my wife, Magdalene, whose encouragement made the many years of study possible, the disciples of the Bread of Life Christian Center and Church, the students, staff and faculty, alumni, and friends of the Bread of Life Bible Institute, Pastors and congregations of the Bread of Life Church Fellowship, whose encouraging response prompted me to write this book. Prayerfully you now have the opportunity to receive the same blessings that were poured out upon all those who heard proclaimed these various truths concerning *godly Spirituality*.

FOREWORD

What a joy to write this foreword. What a blessing came into my life the day I met Jay Leach. He is not only a special friend and companion, but he is also a notable example of what it means to live a godly spirituality.

I have seen the quality of his life close up. During the storms of life, unbearable set backs, and demands of ministry, this very special man of God has stayed the course onward and upward even in the face of adversity.

Marriage carries many roles, commitments, and responsibilities. I have seen Jay fulfill every challenge [a couple that knocked him flat], but, he rebounded with optimism and grace. I observe how our children imitate his qualities and look to him for advice and counsel. Our grandchildren and great grandchildren as well can't get enough of Grandpa.

This love of my life is my husband of forty-nine years, and I thank God for his life. I treat him like a king, and he treats me like a queen!

—Magdalene J. Leach
Wife and Friend

Dr. Magdalene J. Leach, an ordained minister, is the Co-Founder and Executive Vice President of the Bread of Life Ministries International, a Christian equipping and educational ministry training and encouraging Christian leaders and disciples around the world.

INTRODUCTION

Jesus taught His disciples to pray saying, *". . . . Thy kingdom come! Thy will be done on earth as it is in heaven . . ." (Matthew 6:10 KJV)*. We find little difficulty praying, *"Give us this day our daily bread"* and the rest of the prayer with great expectancy. However, knowledge of His will for His kingdom people on earth as found in the Great Commandment and the Great Commission are not properly prioritized and executed within His Christian community. This neglect of God's purpose has created a void in the disciple's spiritual growth process. In many cases this hindrance begins immediately following their water baptism. Unless the local churches develop methodologies to conserve these converts, Satan will encounter little resistance while implementing his deceptive plan to fill this void. He has been successful in causing a large segment of the Christian church to be "drawn away" through biblical ignorance and ungodly spiritualities. Weekly we hear many declarations from excited pastors concerning conversions to Christ, but many are not as excited concerning the conservation of these converts. This is due to little effort made toward providing nurture, doctrinal teaching, and opportunities put forth for the converts to flesh-out the truths of God's Word in practical experience and service. Sadly many converts remain unstable, spiritually deficient and never become fully established mature disciples.

However, our King expects the church to counter this deception by the establishing of convert conservation ministry designed to "teach them." This must include extensive teaching and training in their new spirituality. We are looking forward to living with Jesus in His Eternal kingdom, but meantime He assured us of God's kingdom presence on planet earth; and we can never forget our individual and corporate responsibilities toward His will and His kingdom!

Upon our acceptance of the fact that the kingdom of God is here, We are to heed the priority Jesus set concerning the importance of how those that are His are to respond to His kingdom. He said, *"But seek first the kingdom of God and His righteousness, and all these things shall be added to you" (Matthew 6:33).* The kingdom of God and His righteousness means to desire and submit to God's righteous rule here on earth. Jesus Christ is the model of what God considers typical for the new-creation man or woman of the kingdom (see Ephesians 4:23-24).

Jesus Christ is not only our Savior; He also is the Indwelling One, who by His presence conforms us to His image. He is the firstborn of a family of glorious sons. Notice the following Scripture passages: *But we see Jesus, who was made a little lower than the angels, for the suffering of death crowned with glory and honor, that He by the grace of God, might taste death for everyone. For it was fitting for Him, for whom are all things and by whom are all things, in bringing many sons to glory, to make the captain of their salvation perfect through suffering (Hebrews 2:9-10).*

And we know that all things work together for good to those who love God, to those who are the called according to His purpose. For whom He foreknew, He also predestined to be conformed to the image of His Son, that He might be the firstborn among many brethren (Romans 8:28-29).

But let us also realize that only Jesus can be like Jesus. As we yield to Him in increasing degrees of surrender, and as we abide in Him and let His Word abide in us, He brings forth life that is not, simply "like" His own, but is His very own life! Christ Himself living within us fulfills God's eternal purpose, which is to make us in His image. If we learn to follow our Captain and function by the principles of His kingdom in our daily living, we will function at a much higher level of anointed living, a godly spirituality.

At the beginning of His earthly ministry Jesus recognized the fact that another kingdom was operating here on the earth, the kingdom of Satan, and the two would be in conflict with one another. In Matthew 4:1-11, I believe Jesus set the precedence for us by showing us how we are to interact with both kingdoms. *First* He showed us that He lived to please the Father and likewise, we should live to please Him. The Scriptures reveal how to submit ourselves to God; then resist the devil and he will flee from you (see James 4:7). *Second*, Jesus taught us the "how to" in this kingdom principle through a demonstration of godly spirituality as He met His enemy, "the prince of this world" (John 14:30), and defeated him. Notice, Christ met temptation with the Spirit of God and the Word of God. He lived under the authority of God's Word; and as He spoke the Word the devil had to flee. *Third,* as we are under His authority, Christ has made that same power and authority available to us corporately and individually. As His Church we carry out His commission through the Holy Spirit and the Word of God (see Matthew 28:18-20). We must be consecrated and available vessels. We all do well to remember, God has only a plan A; there is no plan B! Let's make sure we can get it right.

In my purpose for writing this book: *Section one:* reminds us as the children of God, what the Father went through in Christ Jesus to defeat that old enemy of our souls, Satan. Additionally, we will look at what He expected of believers then, and now of us as a positive result of this miraculous outpouring of His saving grace upon us (see Acts 1:8). *Section two:* expounds on the many Christians being *Drawn Away* from the truth of God's Word, "the faith," of Jude 3. Satan attempts to obscure godly spirituality through exploitation of our biblical ignorance, minds seared through the influences of the world, and his seducing spirits' promotion of an ungodly secular worldview. All of his forms are religious, but Christless and include nothing positive concerning the things of God's kingdom. Our national conscience feels very little, if any guilt when we disobey God's Word. Satan is aided through negative images of believers and the church displayed on every hand throughout our secular society. Yet, Christ is building His church without spot! The church He promised to return for! In *Section three,* I shall attempt to show how we are to victoriously and gloriously live and practice true godly spirituality, *[having to do with the connection itself between the human and divine]* through kingdom principles, as Christ's future Bride; in this life "making ready" for His return. Then finally in *Section four,* we will see how the Holy Spirit desires to lead us much deeper into the Word of God; that the church may be edified. I believe the best way to accomplish this is through the ministry of small groups. The Greek word for *edification* means *"stewardship"* and expresses the concept of orderly management of a household. The focus of the Christian's life should be the clear and sound doctrine found in the Word of God, not human speculation. We should continually study the Word, learn to understand the spiritual connections, and pass them on to others. 1 Timothy 1:3-11 explains, there are strange unbiblical doctrines, therefore it is imperative that all Christians be grounded in Christ and the one true and accepted biblical doctrine. There are always two threats to the church, one from the outside and one from the inside. On the outside the threat (secularism) seeks to draw away disciples through conformity and persecution. On the inside false teachers weave human doctrines mainly concerned with secondary things. These deceptions are designed to bind people into their organizations. *"Also of your own selves shall men arise, speaking perverse things to draw away disciples after them" (Acts 20:30).* The content is often esoteric or philosophical. Our society has developed tremendous resources to influence us to accept worldly standards, discarding biblical and moral standards that were once considered normal, and have placed their own self interests above their regard for God's laws. God forbid! Today these strange doctrines are on the increase along with the traditions of their fathers; which cause aggressive quarrels, disputes and do not serve divine edification (see Titus 3:9). God has equipped every born again Christian with the power of the Holy Spirit to fulfill our responsibility of being faithful to

His standards. At the end of the day, those who have maintained the true Word of God as their offense and defense shall be successful in carrying out our Lord's command of evangelism, in spite of Satan's deceptive efforts. Evangelism with its two branches *[conversion and conservation]* is the life sustaining ministry of the church. When vigorously pursued evangelism closes the gap and counters the ungodly spirituality Satan has sown among God's people. The Holy Spirit desires to deepen our relationship with God through the study, meditation, and application of His Word. For a child of God, there is never an end to spiritual learning. We should continually read and study the Bible, learn to understand the spiritual lessons and faithfully pass them on to others (see II Timothy 2:2). At Christ's return will you be ashamed to meet Him? I pray that God in Christ, our true Anchor, will use this book for His glory, allowing a wide-spread reading and heeding by many so they will not be "Drawn Away!"

Jay R. Leach
Fayetteville, NC
www.breadoflifenc.com

SECTION I

CONQUEST
ON THE CROSS

CHAPTER 1

YOUR FIRST LOVE

". . . . You have persevered and have
patience, and have labored for My name's
sake and have not become weary.
Nevertheless I have this against you,
that you have left you first love
Revelation 2:3, 4

The number one priority for those of us who claim Jesus Christ as our Savior and Lord goes right to the heart of godly spirituality: *You shall love the Lord your God with all your heart, with all your soul, and with all your mind.' And, you shall love your neighbor as yourself"* *(see Matthew 22:34-46)*. During the ensuing discourse with Jesus the Pharisees appeared to be trying to trap Him on some controversial theological issue. However, Jesus silenced His enemies by appealing to the Scriptures and quoting Deuteronomy 6:5 and Leviticus 19:18. One's love for God and one's neighbor sums up the Law and the prophets (see Romans 13:8-10). These doctors of the law debated over which of the many commandments was the greatest. Instead of debating as the Pharisees did, we should insure first of all that we are fully obeying God, and truly loving Him and one another, our first love:

No one can love God apart from knowing Jesus Christ as Savior (see John 8:42). And when you know and love God, the love of God will be shared with others. We will share with others because we have hope and *"the love of God shed abroad in our hearts by the Holy Ghost which is given unto us" (see Romans 5:5 KJV)*. He continuously encourages us in our hope in God.

Throughout Scripture we are commanded to celebrate God's presence by magnifying the Lord and exalting His name. Psalm 34:3 says, *"Oh magnify the Lord with me and let us exalt His name together."* In spite of the promotion of individualism today, this Psalm promotes unity, characteristic of godly spirituality. If we are urged to magnify and exalt the Lord together, then those with ungodly spiritualities do not magnify or exalt Him at all; which is fast becoming the norm for many proclaimers today. The proper level of unity is only possible through those who are walking by the Holy Spirit. When believers fail to be obedient in personal prayer and studying the Word of God for illumination; they become weak, vulnerable and are easily *Drawn Away*. They are drawn into one or more of the ungodly forms of spirituality which exists outside the light of kingdom of God principles.

Two Classes of Christians

The Bible identifies two kinds of people in the world, those who are saved [in Christ]; and those who are unsaved [not in Christ]. Sometimes these kinds of people are mistakenly confused with the two classes of Christians in the local churches: those who "walk after the Holy Spirit" and those who "walk after the flesh" or said another way' those who are "spiritual" and those who are "carnal." The carnal person is not the same as the "natural" or (unsaved person); though they are treated as such in too many cases. The carnal man is not expected to be mature in Christ at conversion. By placing their faith in Christ, they are justified. While carnal at this level, it is not expected of them to remain so. As in physical births, the babies are fed milk and it is expected of them to grow thereby; even so in the spiritual birth the new born babes are fed on the milk of the Word; it is expected of them to grow in their faith, through the spiritual growth [maturing] process of sanctification. These distinctions have a direct bearing on the reality of spirituality in the daily lives of saved people. There is the possibility of a great transition for carnal Christians into the reality of true Spirit-filled living. The revelation concerning this reality is confession, repentance, and deliverance. This life is realized only when all of its experiences and blessings are experienced by those faithfully pursuing a God-honoring life of righteousness.

This transition from carnal to spiritual is covered at length in the Word of God. However it can be accessed only through prayerful study and proper nurture and training. It is possible to know the truth and not enter its blessing, on the other hand, it's possible to have some measure of the experiences of it and yet not have known the truth. The church and true godly spirituality has *suffered* greatly from those who have sought to understand its principles through their own personal experiences, irresponsible leadership, and secularly oriented teaching and learning methods; apart from the teaching and revelation of the Holy Scriptures. The danger of this error is obvious and running rampart in this country today as many who are truly not [in Christ] attempt to put their natural spin on spiritual truth. The process of sanctification requires steadfastness *in the faith* [guided by the Word and the Spirit] or you may be drawn through Satan's illusions into living a different worldview entwined with deceptive secular humanistic thought.

Secular humanism, Satan's counter to authentic godly spirituality, continues to work fervently at removing true truth and our biblical worldviews from public view. As Jesus was about to be arrested He prayed to the Father that He would keep His disciples in the world. He pointed out a greatly *neglected truth*; His disciples are <u>not</u> of this world! He requested of the Father, *"Sanctify them by your truth. Your word is truth. As you sent Me into the world, I also have sent them into the world. And for their sakes I sanctify Myself, that they also may be sanctified by the truth" (see John 17:17-19).*

As stated earlier, Jesus was aware that there was another kingdom with *influence* in the world as well as the kingdom of God, the kingdom of the devil (see Matthew 12:26). Every since Satan failed in his desire to displace Jesus Christ in heaven and was kicked out, he has attempted to do so here on earth in the hearts of God's people. Before Jesus left us He demonstrated the kingdom strategy for dealing with Satan and his demons through the power of the Holy Spirit and the spoken Word of God. Any spirituality not supported by this combination of graces is an ungodly spirituality!

Two distinct Kingdoms (Domains)

Jesus went about preaching everywhere that the kingdom of God was at hand. There are some 150 references to the kingdom in the New Testament. In His great lesson on prayer, He taught His disciples to pray saying, *"thy kingdom come! Thy will be done . . . ." (see Matthew 6:10 KJV).* Jesus taught another kingdom principle in this chapter; which is key to our spirituality saying, *"Seek first the kingdom of God and His righteousness, and all these things shall be added to you" (Matthew 6:33).* To seek means we really desire God's righteous rule here on earth (see vv. 9, 10). While these two kingdoms are locked in conflict today please note, Jesus successfully endured temptation from the devil (see Matthew 4:1-11) and assured us that He has overcome him and the world.

The Scriptures say, *"Then the devil, taking Him up on a high mountain, showed Him all kingdoms of the world in a moment of time. And the devil said to Him, "All this authority I will give you, and their glory; for this has been delivered unto me, and I give it to whomever I wish. Therefore, if You will worship before me, all will be Yours" (Luke 4:5-7).* And Jesus answered and said to him, *"Get behind me Satan. For it is written You shall worship the Lord your God, and Him only you shall serve" (v. 8).* Notice in verse eight the word "authority" is used instead of kingdoms. Therefore, we see that Satan is speaking of another entity.

The question arises, "How was Satan able to offer these kingdoms of the world to Jesus?" Jesus Himself acknowledged him as the ruler of this world (see John 12:31; 16:11); Paul called him the prince of the power of the air (Ephesians 2:2) and the god of this world in (2 Corinthians 4:4). The Greek word for world is *kosmou* derived from the word *kosmos,* which means order, arrangement, ornament, and adornment. The moving of entities in the world has a system or operational order to them. I'm sure that every student of Bible prophecy takes notice when a "new world order," which is prophesied in the Scriptures is mentioned among world leaders. Each new day, we see the world being arranged into a new order, but as for as the nations of the earth are concerned, the Bible assures us that Jesus Christ is the ruler of the kings of the earth (see Revelation 1:5). Lest we forget, He is the King of kings and Lord of lords. Give Him praise and glory! The Scripture further states that, *"The earth is the Lord's and all its fullness, the world and those who dwell therein (Psalm 24:1).*

Two World views

Now that we realize that these two kingdoms are in the world, it is obvious after little consideration that they are two completely different realities. Each reality is expressed in the lives of the two separate groups of people therein. Another fact is we live in a pluralistic world. What is obvious and true to you may be "a lie to your neighbor next door." If we don't recognize that, we certainly are naïve and have much to learn about people and today's world. The Scripture says, "The whole world lies in wickedness." We must be redeemed "from this present evil world," not made a part of it.

A well-rounded world view will include answers to each of the following questions:

- What is prime reality? To this question the believer would answer God (see Genesis 1:1), but some people with a different world view would probably say the gods, and still others might speak of the material cosmos.

- Who is man? To this as believers we would answer, man is a personal being created by God in His own image. God created man for the purpose of relationship (see Genesis 1:26-28; 3:8; Isaiah 59:1, 2), yet some other people might speak of a sleeping god, and others a highly complicated electro-chemical machine.

- What happens to man at death? Here we would say as believers we are absent from the body present with the Lord (see 2 Corinthians 5:8), or each person will spend eternity in either heaven or hell; others' view might claim extinction or to return in another existence.

- What is the basis of morality? To the believer, the character of God (see Galatians 5:22-23); but to some other people, the affirmation of men, or actual physical and cultural survival.

- What is the meaning of human history? To this we would answer to realize the will of God and live in communion with Him (see Revelation 4:11; 10:6), while other views might say to the gods, or to make paradise on earth and so forth.

Within various basic world views other views or issues often arise. For instance who is in charge of the world—God, man, or no one at all? Is man alone the maker of values? In a relativistic society with no absolutes it's easy to see an antithesis of thought;

any newscast will bear this out. In the questions and answers above; notice the emergence of a biblical worldview and a satanic secular world view. Considering what has been said thus far; each of us falls into one or the other camps, but not both! Please notice everyone has a world view. If you are one who thinks that you have no world view, well, that thinking is also a world view!

The Secular Worldview

There is a distinctly visible worldview operating in each of the two kingdoms. The secular world view in the kingdom of Satan has its false teachers, philosophers, media interpreters, and religious gurus. These individuals are energized through demonic spirits and influences as they promote the **"works of the flesh"** characterized as sexual sins, sins of false spirituality, sins of temper, and sins of drunkenness (see Galatians 5:19-21). Beware! These ungodly people and practices are becoming bolder in society and even some local churches. The majority of Christians today are not living out God's principles in their families, business relationships and material needs. Our apathy toward sin gives a clear indication of our spiritual condition. Contemporary Christians seem to be helpless to keep their families together. The secular agenda says, "There are no absolutes and therefore everything is relative. No absolutes translate into no God, no truth; so do "your own thing!" "After all truth is up to you, the secularists declare." This attitude is seen in the absenteeism, lack of dedication, commitment, and the unfaithfulness to Christ and His Church. God forbid! The works of the flesh (see vv. 19-21) are evident in those who ignorantly seek perfection through the flesh and self efforts (law) which are:

- adultery
- fornication
- uncleanness
- lewdness
- idolatry

- sorcery
- hatred
- contentions
- jealousies
- outbursts of wrath
- selfish ambitions
- dissensions
- heresies
- envy
- murders
- drunkenness
- revelries and the likes

The Scripture distinctly says, *"Those who practice such things will not inherit the kingdom of God" (Galatians 5:21b).* Notice it said those who practice such things. Paul here is referring to people who have never been born again. These "sins of the flesh" characterize their very lifestyle, because of their sinful nature. Except they be born again in hell they will lift up their eyes. Paul has a similar list in 1 Corinthians 6:9-11, however, here he is warning the backslidden Christians. Should we allow them to continue to operate in the midst [spiritually ignorant] or should we confront them with the truth? I've asked this question because so many of our church leaders are ignoring these people for the sake of numbers, money, or lack of a viable teaching and training ministry. *"Know ye not that the unrighteous shall not inherit the kingdom of God? Be not deceived: neither fornicators, nor idolaters, nor adulterers, nor effeminate, nor abusers of themselves with mankind, nor thieves, nor covetous, nor drunkards, nor revilers, nor extortioners shall inherit the kingdom of God. And such were some of you: but ye are washed, but ye are sanctified, but ye are justified in the name of the Lord Jesus, and by the Spirit of God."(KJV).* The backslider is having trouble with the "flesh." In Galatians 5:24, Paul says, *"And they that are Christ's have crucified the flesh with the affections and lusts."*

So many Christians in the local churches are defeated because they don't understand the fact that they have *two natures [the flesh (human) and the spirit (divine)]*. Think about it, if we feed our spirit on the Word of God like we feed our body physical food, both requiring daily meals the spirit would win over the flesh every day. Feed the spirit and crucify the flesh. You can get an upper hand over your flesh by memorizing and meditating on Scripture verses even beginning with those on this page. Spiritual warfare is in your mind! Renew your mind through the Word (see Romans 12:1-5). Remember the Word of God is alive! I stated earlier, these two natures war against each other (see Galatians 5:17). A thorough teaching on this subject would break many yokes and set many saints free. We can by the grace of God and the power of the Holy Spirit crucify the flesh; but the flesh must be crucified daily! "Therefore let him who thinks he stands take heed lest he fall." "*No temptation has overtaken you except such as is common to man; but God is faithful, who will not allow you to be tempted beyond what you are able, but with the temptation will also make the way of escape, that you may be able to bear it*" (*1 Corinthians 10:12-13*). If you don't already know these verses of Scripture from memory, *memorize them now*, before you read another paragraph. Born again Christians have crucified the flesh with its passions and lusts. Christians have accepted the cross of the Lord Jesus. It is Christ whom the believer has put on by faith—therefore, with Paul we say, "*I am crucified with Christ: nevertheless I live; yet not I, but Christ liveth in me: and the life which I now live in the flesh I live by the faith of the Son of God, who loved me, and gave Himself for me*" (*Galatians 2:20 KJV*).

A happy backslider is one who has confessed his or her sins, repented, and put them out of your life (see 1 John 1:7, 9). Those born of God will not practice such an ungodly spirituality [life]; because the conviction of the Holy Spirit and the *divine* nature within you (see 2 Peter 1:4) will not allow you to remain there. Please note these verses were directed to the Galatians [church]. Agreeing with a secular worldview will lead to the same end experienced by these Galatians. The Dake Annotated Reference

Bible notes suggest the following, "Twenty things wrong with the Galatians":

1. Being so soon removed from Christ (v 6)
2. Permitting false teachers to pervert the gospel (v 7; 5:8-12)
3. Were bewitched from obedience to the gospel of Christ (3:1; 5:7)
4. Were crucifying Christ anew (3:1)
5. Attributing their gospel blessings to the Law of Moses (3:2)
6. Beginning in the Spirit and seeking perfection in the flesh (3:3)
7. Were suffering for the gospel in vain by losing gospel benefits (3:4)
8. Going back to the law of works to be justified (3:10-12; 5:4)
9. Turning back to the weak and beggarly elements of the world (4:9)
10. Desiring to be in bondage (4:9, 21)
11. Going back to observance of Sabbaths and other festivals of the law (4:9-10)
12. Considered Paul an enemy for telling them the truth (4:16)
13. Were zealous for wrong things (4:17-18)
14. Backslidden and in need of rebirth (4:19)
15. Were back in the law of bondage (5:1)
16. Being convinced of circumcision (5:2)
17. Were fallen from grace (1:6; 5:4)
18. Using liberty as an occasion to the flesh to commit sin (5:13)
19. Biting and devouring one another (5:15, 26)
20. Seeking to escape persecution of the cross of Christ (6:12)

The question is raised: How can human beings, who are sinful by nature, win the favor of God, who is holy? The apostle Paul answered, "They cannot!" "*For he that soweth to his flesh shall of the flesh reap corruption; but he that soweth to the Spirit shall of the Spirit reap life everlasting. And let us not be weary in well doing: for in due season we shall reap, if we faint not (see Galatians 6:8-9 KJV). Be not deceived!* The only way to please God is to trust His grace and stop trying to acquire His favor by obedience to the law and works. God's forgiving love *through* Christ is the one and only ground for salvation, and entry into His eternal kingdom. Faith in the *total* sacrificial work of His Son, Jesus Christ and right standing with God requires a new nature, and no one can remake him/ herself.

The Kingdom worldview

The Christian has a *kingdom* or *biblical* world view; which operates from a body of revealed truth gained through the Holy Spirit and the Word of God. Additionally, it is characterized by the person being filled with the Spirit. The Bible unequivocally declares, *"Be filled with the Spirit" (Ephesians 5:18).* In contrast to the persons who live by the works of the flesh, the loyal subjects of the kingdom of God are filled and led by the Holy Spirit and they do what is right [freely] and not by the compulsion [bondage] of the law as is the case of those guided by the flesh. Another contrast, the works of the flesh are *plural,* and the **fruit of the Spirit** is singular, *one and indivisible (see Galatians 5:22-23).* When the Spirit fully controls the life of a Christian [godly spirituality]; he or she produces *all* of these virtues:

The first three concerns our *attitude* toward God:

- Love—The Greek term is "agape" meaning the love of God. This love does not refer to emotional affection, physical attraction, or familial bond. It refers to respect, devotion, and affection that lead to willing, self-sacrificial service, and not necessarily looking for something in return (see also John 15:13; Romans 5:8; John 3:16-17).
- Joy—is happiness based on unchanging divine promises and kingdom realities. It is the sense of well-being

experienced by one who knows all is well in his or her relationship with God. That is, joy in spite of favorable or unfavorable life circumstances (see also John 16:20-22).

- Peace—is the inner calm that results from confidence in one's saving relationship with Christ. Like joy, peace is not related to one's circumstances of life (also see John 14:27; Romans 8:28; Philippians 4:6-7, 9).

The second three deals with *social relationships*:

- Longsuffering—refers to the ability to long endure the frailties, offenses, injuries, and provocations inflicted by others and the willingness to accept irritating or painful people and situations (also see Ephesians 4:2; Colossians 3:12; 1 Timothy 1:15-16).
- Kindness—is tender concern for others reflected in a desire to treat others gently; just as the Lord treats all true Christians (also see Matthew 11:28-29; 19:13-14; 2 Timothy 2:24).
- Goodness—is moral and spiritual excellence manifested in active kindness (also see Romans 5:7; 6:10; 2 Thessalonians 1:11).

The third group describes *principles* that guide a Christian's conduct:

- Faithfulness—is the living, divine principle of inward and wholehearted confidence, assurance, trust, and reliance in God and all that He says (also see Lamentations 3:22; Hebrews 10:19-38; 11:1, 6; Romans 4:17; 8:24; John 3:15; Philippians 2:7-9; 1 Thessalonians 5:24; Revelation 2:10).
- Gentleness—also translated "meekness" is a humble and gentle attitude that is patiently submissive and balanced in tempers and passions and in every offense; while having no desire for revenge or retribution. Psalm 25:9 says,

> *"The meek will He guide in judgment: and the meek will He teach His ways."*

- Self-control—is the restraining in the indulgence of passions and appetites (also see Proverbs 23:1-3; 25:16; 1 Corinthians 9:25-27; Philippians 4:5; 1 Thessalonians 5:6-8; Titus 2:2-3, 11-12; 2 Peter 1:5-6).

No law can condemn one with the fruit of the Spirit; *LAW only condemns sin, not righteousness* (Romans 3:19-20; 7:13; Galatians 3:19). Paul counsels, *"Knowing this, that the law is not made for a righteous man, but for the lawless and disobedient, for the ungodly and for sinners, for unholy and profane, for murderers of fathers and murderers of mothers, for manslayers, for whoremongers, for them that defile themselves with mankind, for men stealers, for liars, for perjured persons, and if there be any other thing that is contrary to sound doctrine" (1 Timothy 1:9-10) KJV.* All true Christians have, *crucified the flesh with the affections and lusts (see Galatians 5:24) KJV.* We live in the Spirit; so let us also walk in the Spirit!

Virtues and Values

The fallout from the two worldviews is a reflection of what is most important to the two kinds of people involved, who foster either life in the Spirit or life in the flesh. The secular view mainly concerns values; while the kingdom view concerns values and virtues. As Christians today, we must be very careful in following to close to the culture. In the culture what is most important seems to focus on (my) individual rights. As the values concerning specific issues are tossed out into the court of public opinion, the Christian must filter each of them through the Word of God, the Holy Bible, before speaking to those issues. One of the greatest ways we can dishonor God is put Him in second place in any area of our life. We have no right to compromise God's truth in order to accommodate some particular violation (s) of the Scriptures. In many cases these values are based on some legislated law enacted in view of some individuals' personal preferences, or those of the court of public opinion, again in violation of God's Word. These secular beliefs, statements, and some legislated laws actually require a change or going against the Word of God and the Christian's kingdom world view, for them to be in agreement. Two examples of the hot issues today are cohabitation and same-sex marriage. How can we vote against the Word of God? In spite of what society says, God's Word settles it for those who are His. The standards of sexual permissiveness that is being taught in America through TV, movies, secular books, the Internet, magazines and even some of our schools' textbooks have destroyed the biblical standards in the majority of the peoples' minds today.

In days gone by, virtues reflected the way of life of the community. Even the unbelievers had to respect them in God's people. Many of us can remember when the doors to many homes were secured with some flimsy home made locking device or just closed. People had respect for one another's property. A fence except for keeping livestock in was an insult in many communities. The above character qualities, [virtues] the fruit of the Spirit is produced in the Christian's new nature by the Holy Spirit. The reality of the fruit of the Spirit is foreign to human nature even when that nature is functioning at its best. Presented here also is a living description of the life that Christ lived while here on earth. Further, it is a statement of the manner of life which He desires Christians to experience here and now. These nine words [virtues] form a biblical definition of what the apostle meant when he said, "For me to live is Christ." Therefore:

- Virtues are distinguishing Spirit-formed quality traits of true godly spirituality.
- Values reflect something highly rated and of moral worth to the individual or group reflecting what he or she believe and practices.
- Virtues are biblically based Christian characteristics of who we are.

- Values seem to be relatively based on societal or culturally determined current issues of worth today; and like carnal Christians, they may change tomorrow!
- To the culture virtues are out and values are in, however, I think both words seem to be evolving in today's society to fit one's personal spirituality.

Not of this world

It seems too good to be true, that God is not angry and waiting for humanity to appease Him. God is a God of love in fact, God is love and He suffered in the death of His only Son by putting the wrath due to us upon Him in order to reconcile humankind to Himself. Those individuals who accept the works of the Son in their hearts by faith are reborn from above (see Romans 10:9-10) and are now in Christ. Christians are no longer of this world, yet they remain in the world (see John 17:14-19). The world hates them because their values are actually counter to the world's values; and therefore the mature Christian does not join in or agree with their sins.

Christ came down born of a virgin and took up an earthly residence; and we who are born of God have taken up a heavenly residence in Christ. Actually Christians are living accusations against the world's immorality. The world follows Satan's secular agenda, and he is the enemy of Jesus Christ and His people. *Therefore if any man be in Christ, he is a new creature; old things are passed away; and behold all things are become new (2 Corinthians 5:17).* As Christians:

- We are brand new people on the inside; with new life given to us by the Holy Spirit. Because Christ died for us, we also are dead to our old life [spirituality].
- We are not reformed, rehabilitated, reeducated or turning over a new leaf—we are re-created (new creations) thinking in union (life) with Christ (see v. 17; Colossians 2:6-7).

- We are brought back by God Himself *(who reconciled us)* by imputing our sins, making Jesus a sin-offering by putting them upon Him on Calvary.
- We are now justified, or made righteous (see Romans 4:24-25). We are no longer enemies, but we have peace with God.
- We are reconciled to God; so we encourage others to do the same, as we have the ministry of reconciliation (vv. 18-19).
- We are trusting in Christ because a divine exchange has taken place—Christ took our sins and gave us His righteousness. Our sins were poured out on Christ at His crucifixion and His righteousness was poured out on us at our conversion. Jesus took what He did not deserve to prevent us from receiving what we do deserve (v. 21). Give Him praise and glory!
- We are sent corporately and individually on behalf of the kingdom of God as Christ's ambassadors to the world with a message of reconciliation. We are not to take this responsibility lightly. Are you fulfilling your assignment as Christ's ambassador?
- We are accountable to Christ as to how we carry out His commission here on earth!

Only through inward virtues instilled by the Holy Spirit and the Word of God can we truly begin to appreciate what God has done for us. Virtues reflect (inwardly) what we are in Christ; while values reflect (somewhat outwardly) what we do or show worth. Our virtues will not always allow us to agree with societal or cultural values.

REFLECTION

*Trust in the Lord with all your heart,
and lean not to your own understanding;
in all your ways acknowledge Him, and
He will direct your paths (Proverbs 3:5-6).*

Review Responses (Chapter 1)

1. The most important thing I learned from this chapter was:

2. The area that I need to work on the most is:

3. I can apply this lesson to my life by:

4. Closing statement of Commitment:

CHAPTER 2

SATAN'S DOUBLE LOSS

When people are tempted and still continue strong,
they should be happy.
After they have proved their faith,
God will reward them with life forever.
God promised this to all those who
Love Him.
James1:12, NCV

Though Satan was able to sway a third of the angels to follow him on his journey from heaven; it was a one way loss for all of them. He is loose but on a leash. He is not free to do as he pleases. He is one of God's created beings and therefore he is limited to what God allows among free-willed humanity here on earth. The Bible says, Satan lurks about as a roaring lion seeking whom he may devour. However, all that Adam lost at the tree of the knowledge of good and evil, Christ took back in His deadly defeat of Satan on the tree on Calvary.

Satan is a defeated foe! Like the older newspaper clippings of "believe it or not" from a by-gone era; it's your choice to accept it as truth or something else. Remember, choices determine eternal destiny. Those who have chosen God's plan are in Christ at the right hand of the Father; and Christ's presence is in them here on the earth. We walk by faith not by sight!

Who is Satan anyway?

To understand who Satan is we will briefly review his past and motivation. The Scripture reveals that Satan, is a created being, and therefore dependent upon God for his very existence (see Ezekiel 28:13, 15). He was at one time Lucifer, one of the most powerful angels in heaven. He was the covering Cherub created with music in his being and placed by God to cover the throne; and therefore responsible for the angelic worship and activities in the heavenly sanctuary (see Ezekiel 28:14-18).

He developed an insatiable desire to become a God like his Creator. He was lifted up in pride over his God-given wisdom, anointing, and beauty (see Ezekiel 28:17; Proverbs 16:18; 18:12; 1Timothy 3:6). He fell through pride and self-will, the very essence of sin (see Isaiah 14:12).

Looking at his activity in Scripture, it becomes evident that the majority of his work centers on deception; however it's important to remember that his activities are limited by God, especially toward His children. We see that clearly in the experiences of Job (see Job 1-2). He is mighty but he is not all-Mighty, he is powerful, but he is not all-Powerful, nor is he Omnipresent. Within his kingdom is a vast host of evil spirit beings, demons, and fallen angels who function as his messengers (see Psalm 78:49; Revelation 12:7-9; Romans 8:38).

His Domain

The Scriptures clearly point out that in the universe and more specifically surrounding the earth, there is a kingdom of darkness. It is the direct opposite of the kingdom of God which is a kingdom of light. Note the contrast of the two kingdoms;

Satan's kingdom

- A kingdom of darkness
- A kingdom of sin and unrighteousness
- A kingdom of sickness and disease
- A kingdom of deception
- A kingdom of sorrow and death

God's Kingdom

- A Kingdom of light
- A Kingdom of holiness and righteousness
- A Kingdom of healing and health
- A Kingdom of truth
- A Kingdom of joy and life

The domain of the kingdom of darkness is where ever Satan exercises dominion. It influences the kingdoms of the world from "the heavenly places" (see Ephesians 2:2; 3:10; 6:12; Revelation 12:3, 7-12). It influences the kingdoms of this *world system* (see Luke 4:5-6; Revelation 11:15; Matthew 8:8-10). His demons attack humans spiritually, morally, mentally, physically, and emotionally seeking to upset their mooring so they will be *drawn away* from the truth (see 1 Timothy 4:1; Mark 13:22; 1 John 2:26). Believers often either ignore Satan's existence and power or overemphasize it. It is important to recognize that he does not exercise authority where God does not allow.

Christ's Victory

Death is the greatest power of Satan manifested, but Jesus conquered it by His resurrection (see Hebrews 2:14; Jude 9: 1 John 3:12; John 8:44). The fact that the Lord Jesus conquered Satan and all his demonic hosts has made complete victory available for every believer. He conquered Satan and his evil in two major realms, personally and representatively.

1. During His wilderness sojourn, He conquered Satan *personally* in the *three* major temptations:

    *   *Body*—the lust of the flesh (Luke 4:2-4)
    *   *Soul*—the lust of the eyes (Luke 4:5-6)
    *   *Spirit*—the pride of life (Luke 4:9-12)

    Therefore, He was tempted in the wilderness in the three areas of man's being: spirit, soul, and body and in the three areas of sin: the lust of the flesh, the lust of the eyes, and the pride of life (see Matthew 4:1-11; Luke 4:1-13; 1 Thessalonians 5:23; 1 John 2:15, 16). Satan tempted the first Adam in these same areas (see Genesis 3:1-3). The first Adam *fell*, thus bringing his entire unborn race under satanic control and into the kingdom of sin, sickness and death. He tempted Jesus in the wilderness seeking to gain dominion over the Last Adam. Jesus Christ was tempted in all points as we are without sin (see Hebrews 2:18; 4:15).

2. He conquered Satan *representatively*, *for us*, at Calvary in His death, burial, and resurrection (see Luke 11:20-22; Psalm 19:5; Isaiah 53:12). Give Him praise!

The Christian and the kingdom of darkness

The Christian must realize all that God has provided for our victory over the power of evil. **We must stand** in our *position, responsibility, battleground* and *our spiritual armor* (see Ephesians 6:10-18) wielded through a renewed mind (Romans 12:1-2); *for the mind is the conduit used to sway the soul for good or evil; therefore it is a battlefield!* We must not be fearful (see 2 Timothy 1:7), but utilize the spiritual weapons provided by Christ's victory. *Lest Satan should get an advantage of us: for we are not ignorant* *of his devices (2 Corinthians 2:11) KJV. For the weapons of our warfare are not carnal, but mighty through God to the pulling down of strongholds; casting down imaginations, and every high thing that exalteth itself against the knowledge of God, and bringing into captivity every thought to the obedience of Christ (2 Corinthians 10:4-5) KJV.* I believe that not since apostolic times have Christians been so challenged with the mind games of Satan through false teachers as they are today. **As Christians we must stand firm on the [foundation]** of all that Jesus Christ is; all that He said; and all that He did! This can only be known experientially as we are identified *with* and *in* Christ. **We are anchored in Jesus.** An anchor is only as secure as to that which it is fastened (see 1 Corinthian 3:11).

1.   The Christian's Position—Legally

- We are in Christ (see Ephesians 1:3-7). In Christ we are partakers of the divine nature (2 Peter 1:4).
- We are new creatures (see 2 Corinthians 5:17; Galatians 6:15).
- We are in the kingdom of light (see Colossians 1:13-14; Romans 8:38; Acts 26:18).
- We are seated in heavenly places in Christ (see Ephesians 1:3; 2:2-8; 6:12).

2.   The Believers Responsibility—Experientially

- The Christian must live victorious over the sins of the flesh, giving Satan no ground to stand on (see John 16:31; Romans 6:7-8; Ephesians 4:27; Galatians 5:22-23).
- The Christian must keep him/ herself in the love of God so that the wicked one will not be able to touch them (see 1 John 4:17-18; 5:18).
- The Christian must submit to God and *then* resist the devil (see James 4:7; 2 Corinthians 2:11).

3. The Christian's Battleground—Personally

- Satan tries to attack the Christian in the three areas of his or her being. He will attack the body and soul to reach the spirit (see 1 Peter 2:11).
- Again, it is a spiritual battle. As we recognize our position in Christ, and fulfill our responsibility; there is no ground upon which Satan can work (see 1 Thessalonians 5:23) *"Do you now believe?"(John 16:31) KJV*.

The audience to whom Jude wrote was vulnerable to heresies and to temptations toward immoral living. He encouraged the Christians to remain *firm* in their faith and trust in God's promises for their future. We too are vulnerable to doctrinal error; we are tempted to give in to sin. Although there is much false teaching around us, we need not fear or give up in despair—*God can keep us from falling!* He guarantees that if we remain faithful, He will bring us into His presence and give us everlasting joy!

> *Now unto him that is able to keep you from falling,*
> *and to present you faultless before the presence of his*
> *glory with exceeding joy, to the only wise God our*
> *Savior, be glory and majesty, dominion, and power,*
> *both now and ever. Amen (Jude 1:24-25) KJV.*

REFLECTION

Pride goes before destruction,
And a haughty spirit before a fall (Proverbs 16:18)

Study Responses (Chapter 2)

1. The most important thing I learned from this chapter was:

2. The area that I need to work on the most:

3. I can apply this lesson to my life by:

4. Closing statement of Commitment:

CHAPTER 3

SET BOUNDARIES

*That you may be blameless and innocent, children of
God without blemish in the midst of a crooked and
twisted generation, among whom you shine as lights in
the world, holding fast to the Word of life
(Philippians 2:15-16) ESV.*

Just as the sun shines at night when the moon is in the right place
of alignment; God shines in darkness when we are in the right
place of alignment with Him. When we are in full view of Jesus,
His love, grace, goodness, and power directly impacts us. In
that place, in that brightness of His presence His light will shine
through us so others can see, no matter how dark the night.

Boundaries

Webster's dictionary defines a boundary as something that marks
or shows a limit or end; a dividing line. Hopefully from what
has been said so far, you have come to the conclusion that there
is a distinct boundary between those Christians who walk after
the Spirit (spiritual) and those who walk after the flesh (carnal);
which actually translates into the mingling of two world views;

seen some times in the same local church. I think that the main reason for this is too much concentration on current events and issues which call for taking sides; and not enough time spent receiving the revealed truth of God's Word. The reality is time spent preaching issues that are of value to you, but may not mean anything to those listening, all this at the expense the true gospel.

The Scripture says, *God, who commanded the light to shine out of darkness, hath shined in our hearts, to give the light of the knowledge of the glory of God in the face of Jesus Christ. But we have this treasure in earthen vessels, that the excellency of the power may be of God and not of us (2 Corinthians 4:6-7) KJV.* God has set boundaries for His children based on the proximity of His Son, Jesus Christ. We can bring hope and life to people and places trapped in discouragement and despair. However, like the moon without the sun has no light; much of what is preached is not the true gospel of Christ and therefore provides no light or life.

Often people try to generate false "moonlight credit" even while knowing they are not the Source. We are just cracked jars reflecting the miracle of the gospel. There is no striving on our part to right the world around us. Only positioning ourselves in the abiding love of Jesus and letting that love shine in and through us. There is no use grabbing the glory when the light of the gospel illuminates the darkness. Some carnal moons continue to try! Every good moon knows full well *their* night light comes from the *Son*!

Jars of Clay

The supremely valuable message of salvation in Jesus Christ has been entrusted by God to frail and fallible human beings ("jars of clay"). What the apostle Paul is emphasizing here is the gist of being a Christian, who walks by the Spirit. He or she does not *focus* on the perishable container but on its *priceless contents,* God's power dwelling in us. Though we are weak, God uses us to spread the Good News, and He gives us power and direction to do it (see Acts 1:8). Knowing that the power is His and not ours, should keep us from pride and motivate us to keep daily contact with Him, our power Source. Our responsibility is to let people see God in and through us. This responsibility is shared by every Christian, so if I am a true Christian I will be guided by the Holy Spirit and the boundaries set by the Word of God; and not what the cultural thinking may be at the moment. The imminent return of Christ should motivate all aspects of our spirituality (our daily life living).

God sets the boundaries

The apostles Peter, Paul, and John along with the other New Testament writers admonish us to leave our old lifestyles and ways of thinking that accompanied our spiritual ignorance; and be holy [separated unto the Lord] in all our conversation [life]. "Be ye holy; for I am holy" (see 1 Peter 1:14) KJV. This means that we cannot compromise morality. Certain immoral acts have become the issues of the day, and couched in such [acts] are sayings such as "he or she has a right to do what they want with their body;' and then there is that old catch all "I'm not harming anybody." Why would we want to be counted with the children of God, but are not willing to obey what the Lord commands in His Word? These individuals find carnal sympathizers within the Christian ranks; and with these allies strive to bring ungodly conformity to the church. In some cases they resort to litigation. It has been said, if you want to find the world look in the church; and if you want to find the church look in the world.

The Scriptures warn that the God of Israel and of the Christian church is holy *and He sets the boundaries or standards for morality.* Unlike the many Christless religious forms across the landscape, Christians are told in the Word of God to be like our heavenly Father—holy in everything we do. He is a God of mercy and justice who cares personally for each of His followers. Our holy God *expects* us to imitate Him by following His high standards for holy living. Christlike qualities in our lives make us different (see Galatians 5:22-23). Our focus and priorities must be His. All of this is in direct contrast to our old ways (see Galatians 5:17-21). We cannot become holy on our own, but God gives us His Holy Spirit and Word to help us obey and He gives us power to overcome sin. The Word of God assures us that we do not have to fall into sin. God's grace and power will free you from sin's power. Turn to Him!

REFLECTION

Happy is the man who finds wisdom,
And the man who gains understanding (Proverbs 3:13)

Study Responses (Chapter 3)

1. The most important thing I learned from this chapter was:

2. The area that I need to work on the most is:

3. I can apply this lesson to my life by:

4. Closing statement of Commitment:

SECTION II

DRAWN AWAY

CHAPTER 4

DRAWN AWAY

But every man is tempted,
*when he is **drawn away** of his own lusts.*
(James 1:14)

Webster's Dictionary defines the word "drawn" to mean, caused to move continuously in certain direction after a force is attached in advance. This describes the carnal Christian. The apostle Paul describes the brethren in Corinth as carnal: *And I brethren, could not speak to you as to spiritual people but as carnal, as to babes in Christ. I fed you with milk and not with solid food; for even now you are still not able to receive it; for you are still carnal. For where there are envy, strife, and divisions among you, are you not carnal and behaving like mere men? For when one says, "I am of Paul," and another, "I am of Apollos," are you not carnal? (1 Corinthians 3:1-4).*

Carnal Christians

Many refer to the people the apostle Paul speaks of in chapter three as natural or unregenerate men. I don't think he would be addressing them as brethren if that was the case. There is a vast difference between the two. The natural person does not have the Spirit of God, in contrast to the Christian who does have the Holy Spirit (see 1 Corinthians 15:44-46). The carnal person is a spiritually immature Christian who is walking by the flesh. In the case of the church at Corinth, the apostle Paul did not expect them to be mature at the time of their conversion or rebirth. However, they had been drawn by the Spirit and united with Christ in His death on the Cross (see Romans 6:3-5); and the Spirit of God had come to live in them (see 1 Corinthians 2:12) and spiritual growth would be expected.

Christians were no longer to live according to the flesh; and they must resist the temptation to settle for a superficial ungodly spirituality. Angels, rituals, and human role models all have their places, but none of them compare with Christ. And therein lays the staggering promise of the gospel; Jesus Christ, who comes to us and offers Himself. Because of His perfect payment for sins, we can find the forgiveness we so desperately need.

Not only that, we can experience eternal life, which Jesus Himself described as an intimate never-ending relationship with God the Father and the Son. Now with that mind-boggling opportunity, why would we look elsewhere or settle for anything less? Yet the Christians at Corinth like many in the local churches today, failed to align with their righteous position in Christ; "for you are still carnal" (v. 2).

Still Carnal

Looking at the line of notable pastors who had served this great church at Corinth, undoubtedly like so many Christians do today; these converts being drawn away found themselves satisfied with their present position (just saved). This topic is fully explored in chapter 18. God justifies us at conversion, but we have a say concerning our rate of progression in the process of conservation [sanctification] and growth toward maturity. Therefore, many remain infants when they should be spiritually mature and able to distinguish the antithesis between good and evil. In Hebrews 5:14, we are told:

> *But solid food belongs to those who are of full age;*
> *that is, those who by reason of use have their senses*
> *exercised to discern both good and evil.*

I'm sure that we can see ourselves reflected in these Christians at Corinth. They did not necessarily lack the truth concerning righteousness, they lacked *[experience]* in practicing the truth they had. Maturity comes through "practice" and "application" of truth. Those who follow God's will by obeying the Spirit and the Word of God mature in the faith and are able to distinguish good and evil.

Church Discipline

Many sins such as reveling, conceiving babies out of wedlock, cohabitation, same sex marriages, and unions are very quickly becoming the societal norm, even in the so-called Bible belt area of this country. As many members of the local churches seem for some reason to not desire sanctification or holiness; the leadership remains accountable to Christ to insure that the truths of God's Word on the various subjects and issues are taught and adhered to [make disciples!]. Though many of the issues today are sanctioned by our national officials; they violate the truth of God's Word; and the church ceases to be an authentic church if it legally and intentionally affirms something that plainly violates Scripture. If the church fails to counter this political move of Satan, then more and more people inside our congregations will be drawn into this error of living. God set the foundations of [marriage and family, the home] from the beginning; we cannot just standby and allow people for whatever motivation destroy them. The Scripture admonishes, *"We ought to obey God rather than men" (see Acts 5:29).* Believers need to vote for the candidates at all levels who best represent the interests of God's kingdom instead of sticking to a particular party. You must have the peace of God in your heart when leaving the polling booth (study Romans 13). The church must listen to the Spirit and go on to maturity overcoming this ungodly attitude and atmosphere. We now have the love of God, nature of God, the fear of God, and the Word of God cleansing us and bringing us into maturity.

Like the apostle Paul, church leaders cannot allow space for non-biblical gray areas, carnal thinking or worldly counsel concerning the single or married Christian. He addressed the fornication issue in 1 Corinthians 5, 6, and 7. Church discipline must be addressed and adhered to today or the invasion of the flesh will establish a beachhead within our churches resulting in many being *drawn away*. The idea expressed in these chapters is the danger of allowing just a little sin (leaven) to remain in the church due to engrafted ungodly societal or cultural thought. In a little while the little leaven will spread throughout the whole loaf. Many of our churches are so lax today on requirements for church membership that people can slip through without actually being born of God. If not spiritually detected these individuals will one day become deacons or stewards, and lead organizations within the church. The kingdom of God on planet earth does not refer to the future reign of Christ, but to Christ's present rule in the hearts of His people. Unsaved, non-spiritual people have no place or part in the kingdom of God. This reality guaranteed that Paul had the power to expose and discipline those who afflicted the Corinthian church. Christ rules today through bold godly leaders!

Unchallenged sin can soon contaminate the whole church. The sexual offender in this case (see 1 Corinthians 5:1-5), was guilty of sin but the whole congregation was also guilty of ignoring the individuals' disobedience and failing to hold them accountable. This lifestyle can be countered through small group or other people-centered and corporate spiritual-life helping and accountability ministries. Paul was doubly upset because the Corinthians had a twisted view of grace and became proud of their tolerance of this sin. Christ said to the church of the Laodiceans, *"I know thy works, that thou art neither cold nor hot: I would thou wert cold or hot. So then because thou art lukewarm, and neither cold nor hot, I will spue thee out of my mouth. Because thou sayest, I am rich, and increased with goods, and have need of nothing . . ." (Revelation 3:15-17) KJV.* Notice unlike the other six churches which were named by their city location, this church was identified as the people's church (the Laodiceans).

Blinded by their extravagance, the church of the Laodiceans *could not see* their need. But Jesus continued, *"And knowest not that thou art wretched, and miserable, and poor, and blind, and naked" (Revelation 3:17) KJV.* Notice again our word *"drawn"* and its definition, *"to cause to move continuously toward or after a force attached in advance."* I think that in this case we could add *rejecting* [guidance or control]; which are actually two of the many promises that Jesus said the Holy Spirit would accomplish in and for us. Now He is in us! However, many within the church have made the church a vulnerable prey to many other sins of the flesh today by incorporating ungodly cultural norms (see Romans 1:21) in violation of the truths of God's Word such as:

Idolatry—Graven images are obvious but,

- These idols that Christians are worshipping are so subtle, we fail to recognize them.
- We are idolizing the good things God has given us instead of worshipping the Giver. For example, some worship their ministry and others the church building.
- The idol of tolerance is making inroads in many of the local churches as they like the Corinthian church, take pride in their ability to tolerate the influence of ungodly cultural norms, and unsaved, talented sinners. All in order

to fill the ranks of their praise and worship teams, choirs, boards and many of the church's committees.

Money—the love of it,

- The contemporary lust today is more, give me more!
- Many have been blessed with money and they claim God gave them the money to bless others; but when comparing their earning with their giving, it's a joke!
- When money rather than God becomes a person's reason for living, he or she has moved into idolatry.

David said to Araunah, "Neither will I offer burnt offerings unto the Lord my God of that which cost me nothing" (2 Samuel 24:24). In other words, David was saying, my gifts to God are going to cost me something. After all that my wonderful Lord has done for me, I want to give Him something that will represent my hard work and effort. My object of worship is the living God and not the fruits of my labor. Money is a tool. It sustains us physically and can be used to reach souls for Christ. *But money must not be an object of worship.*

Status—another god of this generation expressed, when:

- "I achieve a higher position and then I will share Christ with others." "I'll be respected and therefore others will listen to my message."
- Christian leaders are not going unaffected by this god of status. I've sat with some of them in their churches and listen as they give the financial worth on some of their members or their profession. They place great emphasis on status.

Higher Knowledge—The Bible says, "Knowledge puffeth up" (see 1 Corinthians 8:1) KJV.

- I thank God for educated teachers, and learned men and women. But it should never cause us to be cynical, puffed up, proud, or arrogant.
- Paul said, "I count my life as dung that I might win Christ." Paul was a learned man (see 2 Corinthians 11; 2 Timothy 2:15).

Leaving a carnal lifestyle

As born again Christians and under the conviction of the Holy Spirit, we should not desire this carnal lifestyle. However, the only effective way out is God's way. King David said to God, *"Wash me thoroughly from mine iniquity, and cleanse me from my sin . . . . Create in me a clean heart, O God; and renew a right spirit within me" (see Psalm 51:2, 10)*. God's plan consists of two steps out of the carnal into the spiritual. The two steps are confession and repentance of our sin.

Confession

One of the problems among many Christians today is that they want to give *partial confessions* [confession means agreeing with God and His Word about anything or matter]. In light of this definition, how should we treat this sin in the church? Perhaps an example from early church will drive home the seriousness of trying to alter God's Word and purpose. In the case of Ananias and Sapphira a husband and wife team; who sold a possession for a certain price and kept back part of the price for themselves. When Ananias brought the money to the apostles, he laid it at their feet as though it was the total amount.

Then Peter said, "Ananias, Satan has filled your heart. When you claimed this was the full price, you were lying to the Holy Spirit. The property was yours to sell or not, as you wished. And after selling it, it was yours to decide how much to give. How could you do a thing like this? You weren't lying to us, but to God" (see Acts 5:3-4) TLB. The Bible says when Ananias heard this he fell down dead. I don't believe the problem was that they only gave part of the money, as would probably be with many Christians today; I think God was upset because of their half truth—their half confession. Later on in the passage, Sapphira also told half a story; and like Ananias, she too, fell dead at the apostle's feet.

Complete confession is God's way of cleaning us up. God's Word says, *"If we confess our sins, He is faithful and just to forgive us our sins, and to cleanse us from all unrighteousness" (1 John 1:9).* Confession frees us to enjoy fellowship with Christ. However, some Christians feel so guilty that they confess the same sins over and over. Other Christians believe that God forgives them when they confess, but if they died with unconfessed sin, they would be lost. Certainly neither of these Christians possesses and shows the joy of fellowship with Christ as they should; in fact they are poor and misleading witnesses for true godly spirituality.

When we come to Christ, He forgives all the sins we have committed or will ever commit. We don't need to confess the sins of the past all over again; thank God they are under the blood of Jesus! Of course we should continue to confess our sins, but not because failure to do so will make us lose our salvation. Our relationship with Christ is secure [we are justified through the blood of Christ]. So, we must confess our sins [now that we are saved] so that we can enjoy the fullest fellowship and joy with Him.

True confession also involves a *commitment* not to continue in sin, if it was our intention to go and commit that same sin we have not genuinely confessed, we are yet carnal!

Repentance

To really come out of a carnal lifestyle God's way, we must take the next step of repentance. Repentance means to:

- Agree with God that our sin truly is sin and that we are willing to turn from it fully (180 degrees anything less does not count as true repentance!).
- Insure that we come clean and not try to conceal our sins from God and consequently from ourselves.
- Recognize our tendency to sin. Be open and transparent in all you do. Admit your weakness to God. *Trust Him* to cleanse, forgive and keep you by His grace and mercy.

Sin in the life of the Christian breaks fellowship but does not destroy our sonship. God provides for the sins of the saints through the heavenly ministry of Christ. We are saved from the penalty of sin by His death (see Romans 5:6-9), and we are saved from the power of sin by His life (Romans 5:10). The Holy Spirit represents Christ to us on the earth, and the Son represents us to God in heaven. He is our Advocate meaning "One who pleads our case." The Christian who truly understands God's provision for a life of holiness does not want to deliberately disobey God. Jesus said, *"If anyone loves Me, he will keep My word; and My Father will love him, and we will come to him and make Our home with him" (John 14:23).* "Anyone" [you can't get more personal than that!]. To prevent being drawn into carnality, we must be "full of the Spirit," continually (see Ephesians 5:18), then we will yield to the Spirit of truth whom Jesus promised would guide us into all truth (see John 16:13). The Spirit's guidance and control will stabilize us and make us fit for the Master's use.

No true fellowship without love

The major conflict between the kingdom of God and Satan's kingdom shows up in the area of love; which will either be shown for the Father or for the world, [by definition all that belongs to this life that is opposed to Christ]. As stated earlier it is Satan's system in society opposed to God and trying to uproot His kingdom.

If we love the world we lose the love of the Father and cease to do His will. Anything in our lives that will *draw us away* from our love for God and His spiritual things; or makes it easy for us to sin is *carnality* and must be put away. There can be no true fellowship without love. Unless we love God and His children, we cannot walk in the light of fellowship with God; and therefore our spirituality is faulty. Don't be *drawn away!*

REFLECTION

The fear of the Lord is the beginning of wisdom,
and the knowledge of the Holy One is understanding
(Proverbs 9:10)

Study Responses (Chapter 4)

1. The most important thing I learned from this chapter was:

2. The area that I need to work on the most is:

3. I can apply this lesson to my life by:

4. Closing statement of Commitment:

CHAPTER 5

GODLY TRANSFORMATION

He has delivered us from the power of darkness and conveyed us into the kingdom of the Son of His love, in whom we have redemption through His blood, the forgiveness of sins (Colossians 1:13-14).

Transformation begins with *knowing* what salvation is and what it does for us. Many people have a narrow view of salvation. They see it as a way of escaping the consequences of sin; and repentance as a striving or working toward moral purity (holiness). Therefore, they believe that asking Jesus to save them and trying to live good clean lives, equates to a reservation to heaven. This belief is widespread and many are drawn away because of it. First of all accepting Christ is only the first phase of salvation, we are expected to grow to maturity (full discipleship) in our Christian experience; that includes deliverance from the power of sin. It's more than just saying the Sinner's Prayer and that's it. We must allow the forgiveness; healing, prosperity, and transformation of the Holy Spirit to penetrate our whole being and every area of our lives. Proper perspective here gives Christians their greatest hope and joy.

Salvation

Salvation comes from the Greek word *soteiron*, meaning to rescue, deliver, bring to safety, and liberate. The Scripture says, *"If you confess with your mouth, the Lord Jesus, and believe in your heart that God raised Him from the dead, you will be saved." "It is with your heart that you believe and are justified, and with the mouth that you confess and are saved" (Romans 10:9-10) NIV.* These beautiful passages answer the question of salvation. Yet some people think that it's such a complicated process, but that's not the case at all. So if we believe in our hearts and confess with our mouths, the Lord Jesus, we will be saved.

So looking at the definition it's as if our salvation [in Christ] has rescued us from the kingdom of darkness (we are in Christ, saved and *justified*). I don't think we put as much emphasis on just what happens here in reference to what Jesus has actually done for us—**sin demands death** and because of Adam this death penalty includes every person born into this world except Jesus Christ, who was sinless. The Scripture declares, *""For there is no difference; for all have sinned and fall short of the glory of God (Romans 3:23).* Further, *"For the wages of sin is death, but the gift of God is eternal life in Christ Jesus our Lord" (Romans 6:23).* Each of us deserves death and really within ourselves, there is absolutely nothing we can do to save ourselves from this death!

God could have left us in that state, but He didn't, praise God! He fixed the problem by coming to earth Himself, born of a virgin who had known no man. He was born of the Holy Spirit and therefore without the sinful blood of Adam. Because sin demands death, Jesus had to die in our place; that was His purpose in coming. The perfect Lamb! The Scripture says, *"When we still without strength, in due time Christ died for the ungodly. For scarcely for a righteous man will one die; yet perhaps for a good man will one die. But God demonstrates His own love toward us, in that while we were still sinners, Christ died for us. Much more then, having now been justified by His blood, we shall be saved from wrath through Him. For if when we were enemies we were reconciled to God through the death of His Son, much more, having been reconciled, we shall be saved by His life. And not only that, but we also rejoice in God through our Lord Jesus Christ, through whom we have now received the reconciliation"* (Romans 5:6-11). God loves us just the way we are, but He loves us too much to leave us the way we are (see John 15:16; Philippians 1:6).

The moment a person trusts in Christ, that person receives the Holy Spirit (see Romans 8:9), who *constantly* leads, guides, and encourages them in their hope in God. Therefore, in that same light (the Holy Spirit must deliver us, *sanctify us*) to the safety of the next sphere of the marvelous light of salvation [delivered from the power of sin]. While it's one movement, sanctification is a process consuming the rest of our lives on earth. Sanctification is a transformation. Christ alone saves sinners; and only He can give power in the heart to transform us into kingdom citizens, who shines forth as the sun with kingdom influence. Jesus used a very appropriate parable to illustrate this state in our salvation. He said, *"Again, the kingdom of heaven is like a merchant seeking beautiful pearls, who, when he has found "one" pearl of great price, went and sold all he had and brought it."* No matter how a person is led to Christ's kingdom, its values and graces will be beyond estimation. Salvation then is revealed to those who are willing to give up everything to possess it. The kingdom of heaven is righteousness, peace and joy in the Holy Ghost (Romans 14:17). Though we are now at peace and reconciled to God; we have much to do with the progress and successful completion of our journey.

In my younger years, my hobby was restoring and selling old "Volkswagen Beetles." Occasionally I would agree to restore one for someone else. I would let them know that the job was mine entirely doing the work was my joy. Sometimes one of the owners would insist on doing something. Change the tires or something! One day while I was out buying replacement parts, one owner did set out to remove the wheels of his VW. The wheel lug nuts were so tight after being exposed to rust and the elements; that he only rounded off the heads of most of the lug nuts before he gave up; so now the lug wrench was practically useless. When I arrived—he said, "I'm sorry, I thought . . . ." I had a little five pound hammer that I kept close by just for such a particular task. I showed him just how easy the task could have been with the proper tool and know how. I landed one or two heavy blows with that hammer flat on the head of the remaining lug nuts; which broke the corrosion and rust loose enough; then I easily removed them with the lug wrench. Those that he rounded off caused a loss of time that could have been spent productively elsewhere on the job. This one infraction extended the completion time by hours. Each of us is a work in progress. Jesus began the work let's let Him finish it! How much time are you wasting on your life trying to do God's work?

The Master Restorer

When our children were small, [until I wised up] for some reason I would end up late at night on Christmas eve or early Christmas morning trying to assemble their bicycles or other toys. Many times I didn't have time [or take the time] to read the instructions; and on occasion I would end up with the toy together, but one or two bolts, screws or some little part left over. Of course on the child's first road test I found out how crucial to the whole operation that little part, now in my tool box along with the screws and bolts really was. Sometimes the damage was irreparable requiring a completely new part; all of this grief because I did not take the time to read the manufacturer's instructions.

God has given us the perfect manual for our whole spirit, soul, and body, the Holy Bible. Sometimes on Christmas day I'd see a child or two with brand new bicycles or other toys with, broken chains, and lights or other accessories missing simply because dad or whoever assembled it did not begin the assembly process in time or simply refused to read the manufacturer's manual; and the end result was a broken-hearted little girl or boy.

In the local church we tend to compartmentalize our lives into physical, mental, and spiritual or (body, soul, and spirit). The fact of the matter is a proper biblical worldview, properly ordered, and unified, concerns the whole person in whom these parts are not separate entities, but are interconnected. First Thessalonians 5:23 says, *"Now may the God of peace Himself sanctify you completely; and may your whole spirit, soul, and body be preserved blameless at the coming of our Lord Jesus."* Here we see that God's interest in sanctifying is not limited to the transformation of part of a person, but the whole person.

When we check the Creator's manual, the Holy Bible, we'll find ways of dealing with the whole person. We'll notice in the temptations Satan began with the body, appealing to the eye; then he worked on through the soul and then he got to the *weakened* spirit. However, God's kingdom order begins with spirituality. Finally, He works through our spirit (inside out) to align our soul and body. This godly transformation is from the inside out! Any other order begins in the flesh and ends in the flesh. Notice what Jesus had to say of the Pharisees who had an external change only, *"Woe unto you, scribes and Pharisees, hypocrites! For ye make clean the outside of the cup and of the platter, but [within] they are full of extortion and excess"* (Matthew 23:25). He continues, *"Woe unto you, scribes and Pharisees, hypocrites! For ye are like unto whited sepulchers, which indeed appear beautiful [outward] but are within full of dead men's bones, and of all uncleanness"* (v. 27). Jesus condemned the Pharisees and other religious leaders for outwardly *appearing* to be holy but inwardly they remained full of corruption and greed. Living our spirituality merely as a show to others is like washing a cup on the outside only. When we are clean on the inside, our cleanliness on the outside won't be a façade. Ceremonially clean on the outside, the Pharisees still had corrupt hearts. Like the man with the lug wrench and myself not heeding the instructions before proceeding, no matter how great the job may appear it is incomplete [claiming ignorance is no excuse] just because "I did it my way." What a disaster when this applies to hypocrisy in the church; as we will readily see later in this study.

One of the Holy Spirit's tasks in us is to lead us and guide us into truth. If we don't read and study the Bible through which truth is revealed, we round off the lug nuts and have parts left over when we should be through with the job. Some Christians put everything into their personal literal interpretation of the Word of God; which can lead to error. The combination of the Holy Spirit and the Word of God works the work in and through us.

A New Way of Thinking

A Christian without a renewed mind is like a tornado; you can't begin to assess its damage many times until it has totally dissipated or moved from the area. Though we are saved, the process is not over until we are either transformed or conformed. Romans 12:2 leaves no doubt about that when it tells us to *"Be transformed by the renewing of your mind"* which means to be totally committed to the ideals of the kingdom of God; and there by proved [by practice] in everyday life, godly transformation, that God's will for us is good, acceptable and perfect. To be *conformed to this world* means accepting the pattern of the world's systems whose god is, the devil. The Scripture says of those conformed, *"whose minds the god of this age has blinded, who do not believe, lest the light of the gospel of the glory of Christ, who is the image of God, should shine on them" (2 Corinthians 4:4).* These people *choose* not to believe; thereby, opening themselves up to an ungodly spirituality influenced by the god of this world, in their thinking. Proverbs 32:7 says, *"As a man thinks in his heart so is he."*

As Christians, once our spirit is fully under the control of the Holy Spirit our renewed mind as a conduit places our soul in proper alignment under the control of our spirit and the body follows; this is God's proper order! Any guidance of the Holy Spirit concerning the conduct and behavior of the soul and body will be in tune with God's will. So it's reasonable that we would offer our bodies a living sacrifice, holy, acceptable to God.

Even in appealing to reason it just doesn't make sense to consider any other act of consecration, then this supreme service. Therefore, from now on we regard no one according to the flesh, meaning from an external evaluation viewed from an earthly perspective (see 2 Corinthians 5:16a). Our identification in Christ by faith makes existence as a new creation possible (see 2 Corinthians 5:17). Godly spirituality has no indwelling sin! Give God praise and glory! *There is therefore now no condemnation to those who are in Christ Jesus, who do not walk according to the flesh, but according to the Spirit (Romans 8:1). Therefore, brethren, we are debtors not to the flesh, to live according to the flesh. For if you live according to the flesh you will die; but if by the Spirit you put to death the deeds of the body, you will live. For as many as are led by the Spirit of God, these are the sons of God (Romans 8:12-14).*

REFLECTION

My son, if you receive my words, and treasure my commands within you, so that you incline your ear to wisdom, and apply your heart to understanding . . . . Then you will understand the fear of the LORD (Proverbs 2:1-2, 5).

Study Responses (Chapter 5)

1. The most important thing I learned from this chapter is:

2. The area that I need to work on the most is:

3. I can apply this lesson to my life by:

4. Closing statement of commitment:

CHAPTER 6

THE CHRISTIAN'S SPIRITUALITY

Now that you are obedient children of God do not
live as you did in the past. You did not understand,
so you did the evil things you wanted. But be holy in
all you do, just as God, the One who called you, is
holy—"You must be holy, because I am holy"
(1 Peter 1:14-16 NCV).

There is a great deal of confusion concerning a godly Christian's spirituality today. A number of those reared in the Christian faith along with those outside are finding it difficult to accept many traditions of men falsely paraded as godly spirituality. Then, there are those who are settling for an eclectic ungodly spirituality consisting of a mixture of various characteristics and tenets selected from several religious spiritualities. For example, some time ago the cover story of a *Newsweek* magazine titled "Spirituality in America" and bearing the subtitle, "What we believe, how we pray, where we find God," defines spirituality as the "passion for an immediate, transcendent *experience* with God.

The article went on to explain how this transcendent experience is realized in various religions such as Islam, Buddhism, Humanism, the New Age religions, even Environmentalism, Secularism, and many other isms. The writers make no real distinction between the story and vision of each of these religions. Their conclusions seem to be describing all spiritualities as *the search for experience.*

I'm sure that all of us agree that spirituality has an experiential dimension, but the experience is always in keeping with the story from which it arises. So the Christian experience will differ from that of Islam, Buddhism, Jehovah Witnesses, New Age religions, and Secularism because they are all based on different stories. Sometime ago, I read a newspaper article about a spirituality located in the Northwest U.S. called "Chrislam," a supposedly merging of a Christian church and an Islamic Mosque into a single congregation. Groups such as this tend to be ecumenical, which means they put unity ahead of biblical principles. The general focus of those who support this mind-set is to water down the Gospel for the sake of cultural accommodation. First of all Christianity is life in our Lord and Savior, Jesus Christ; while Islam is a religion which casts Christ as a prophet under Mohammed; and that is actually like trying to mix oil and water. Each has its own foundational story. This book is about God's story and the godly spirituality of His people that proceeds from it, and how that spirituality must be maintained in today's anti-Christian, relativistic world where spirituality is considered a common, non-content experience of otherness.

Today we hear much about a search in conjunction with spirituality. Many people have traveled the world over trying various religions, rituals, and practices in search of "the" spirituality or faith. Jude 3 admonishes us to earnestly contend for *the faith* which was once delivered [for all] to the saints. The faith referred to here is not the personal belief in Christ for salvation; here it means the body of teaching [the Bible] passed down in the church by the apostles. In verses 17-22 we read, *but you beloved, remember the words which were spoken before by the apostles of our Lord Jesus Christ: how they told you that there would be mockers in the last time who would walk according to their own ungodly lusts. These are sensual persons, who cause divisions, **not having the Spirit.*** He is saying; above all maintain your life with God. *But you, beloved, building yourselves up on your most holy* *faith, praying in the Holy Spirit, keep yourselves in the love of God, looking for the mercy of our Lord Jesus Christ unto eternal life.*

Today we witness in the media, society at large, and even in some local churches many attacks on the central truth of the Scriptures. Those pertaining to God, Christ, and salvation by God's grace through faith receive special attention. Jude points out that absolutely nothing has been or is being observed about false teachers that should take any Christian by surprise. The apostles had given ample warning (vv. 17-19) that in the last days evil deceivers will come. Notice they are referred to as mockers indicating that one of their main tactics to gain credibility was to tear down godly leaders. He declares that the false teachers are without the **Spirit,** leaving no doubt as to which kingdom or worldview they truly embrace. They are merely worldly unregenerate persons who do not belong to God's kingdom. Jude goes on to tell us how to keep ourselves in the love of God. How, by cultivating our love for Christ, the foundation of godly spirituality, for we cannot be separated from His love for us (see Romans 8:35-39).

Where do we start?

The heart of godly spirituality is *our mystical union with God accomplished by Jesus Christ through the Holy Spirit.* God unites with humanity in His saving *incarnation, death, and resurrection.* We unite with God as we receive <u>our new lives in Christ</u> (see John 3:3; II Corinthians 5:17, 21). A Christian's spirituality then, simply put, is *God's passionate union with him or her and that individual's passionate union with God.* These two aspects of the Christian's spirituality are like the two sides of a single coin—together, not capable of being separated or divided, and unable to exist apart. On one side we find the *divine initiative,* [referring to what God does to make us spiritual]. On the other side we find *our response,* [referring to our reception of the union]. These two sides of a single coin tell us that *God makes us spiritual, and we live the spiritual life.* But to understand these two aspects of spirituality, we must place them in the setting of God's story of the world.

What is God's Story?

It is the story of God's *purposes* for humanity and the world. God created us in His image and likeness, to live in union with Him, to be what He created us to be, and to do what He created us to do: take dominion of the world and make it the place of His glory.

But we failed both of these assignments. We rebelled against God and sought the meaning of life by following the course of evil [deceived by Satan] in our personal choices, plunging the world into a place of violence, greed, and lust. Therefore the resulting predicament in which we find ourselves [we *can change* neither ourselves nor the world]. *So God does it for us. Give Him all praise and glory!*

God's story is the story of how He *reversed* the human condition, broke the hold of sin and death [which separates us from God] and *restored us* to the original vision of becoming the person God created us to be and making the world the place of God's glory. The Christian's godly spirituality, then, does not fall into that described in *Newsweek;* a non-content "transcendence experience" but is God's gift of a *redirected life* in union with His purpose for life. Herein lay the uniqueness of the Christian experience, (God reached down to humanity) as compared to Christless religions, (humanity trying to reach up to God):

Christian Experience by grace (see Ephesians 2:5)

- Humanity in sin (Romans 3:23; 6:23)
- God's initiative reaches down to humanity (Romans 5:8; John 3:16)
- Human response results in a redirected life (see John 3:3-6; 1 John 5:13-15)

Religious Experience by works (see Titus 3:5)

- Humanity in sin (Romans 3:23; 6:23)
- Man's initiative reaches up to God (John 3:18, 36; Ephesians 2:9)
- Human response is futile (Ephesians 2:8-10)

The problem of the Christian's Experience in Spirituality

A major hindrance to the Christian's experience centers on individualism. This problem resulted from an over emphasis on personal salvation; leaving too much un-said and therefore un-done about the gospel. It fails to move from the death of Christ to the victory of Christ over the power of evil. The problem of individualism then breaks out into two streams:

First it produces:

- A spirituality that is reduced to a personal and privatized experience.
- A spirituality that fails to express that Christ has bound, dethroned, and will destroy all evil at the end of history.
- A spirituality in which all of the recapitulation of the work of the second Adam is reduced to "*my* new birth," "*my* version of heaven and hell."
- A spirituality wherein the place of a kingdom community under the reign of God along with the prophetic destiny of humanity is not a part of the message. God's story is incomplete *unless* Christ's incarnation, earthly life, death, burial and resurrection are fully incorporated into the total church and its theology.

Second it produces:

- A Christian spirituality focusing only on the change accomplished in the individual. *You* are saved. *You* are a new person. *You* have been born again.
- A Christian spirituality centering almost exclusively on the individual does not adequately emphasize the role of the church.
- A Christian spirituality that does not realize that at conversion, a convert has only begun the process of being saved in totality.
- A Christian spirituality that does not recognize that the church is the community in which this process is encouraged and brought to fruition.
- A spirituality wherein baptism is seen as *my witness to my salvation*. The divine work of baptism is often neglected. The biblical meaning of baptism is that through identification with Christ we are called to put to death *everything* that is *sin* in our lives and bring to life a new person shaped in the image of Christ by the power of the Holy Spirit (see Romans 8:12-17; 6:22).

  Baptism is not a once and for all *my* witness to the world event. It is a ritual that initiates us into the body of Christ and begins our lifelong pursuit of holiness which takes place in the accountability of God's community on earth, the church (see 1 Corinthians 12:12-26; Hebrews 10:25).

The individualization of many Christians' spirituality has separated the experience and obedience from Christ and the church introducing a cult of easy, entertaining and attractive, something that I call churchanity [false or ungodly spirituality in the church]. However, our major emphasis must not be to make Christianity attractive and entertaining; instead we must emphasize the cost of discipleship, the absolute claim of God over our entire life (see Luke 14:26-28), the necessity of a faith that issues forth in obedience and our belonging to an alternative culture shaped by the kingdom of God.

Another reason for the separation between spirituality and obedience can be found in "cultural conversions." What do I mean? Well, a person may make a radical break from a former way of living into a particular form of Christianity. For example, a person may be persuaded to give up bad habits and join a group whose identity is strongly defined by the absence of smoking, drinking, gambling, etc. The problem is that the new convert may confuse obedience to the forms of this "new culture" with obedience to Christ. The person may be told that obedience means giving up bad habits and taking on *new habits,* such as Bible reading, prayer, witnessing, church attendance and tithing. As good as these new habits may be, they do not reach the heart of Christian obedience and reduces the Christian life to these few principles while obscuring deeper issues. This leads those converts who obey them to *substitute* cultural change of habits for a more far reaching biblical transformation of lifestyle. This leads the convert to enter the Christian life with second hand convictions, which are not his or her own personal convictions. God forbid! This malady sends many of our young people away to college, the military or life choices in general with a sandy foundation, and completely unprepared. Our children must be led to Christ and enabled with a solid biblical worldview, with which to counter the anti-Christian atmosphere that they will find themselves in for the rest of their natural lives.

Society today is not only anti-Christian, but it is also anti-gender. Normally, this would cause us to think of the work place and other cultural professions; but no parent would ever imagine sending their children off to institutions, even some of them religious; where the restrooms and showers have evolved from being marked "Ladies" and "Gentlemen" to "Men" and "Women" to "Both." Today many "restrooms" and "showers" are equipped with swinging doors and no gender signs. This requires a more committed relationship with Jesus Christ, a through personal knowledge of Who He is, and the biblical realization that it is totally impossible to survive without Him!

In another instance, an ungodly spirituality is sneaking into our society through forced multiculturalism by infiltrating education, government at all levels and any other institutions that will allow it, even the church. How is this being accomplished? It is an established fact—Christianity is a life not a religion! Christianity is exclusive, while religion is inclusive and cultural. The powers knowing this to be true actually use it as a tool to ban the Christianity and godly spirituality from the public square; they seem to get away with it because Christianity transcends and transforms culture. Therefore, the door is left open for any Christless spiritualties, hybrid religions, secular beliefs, and practices within the "culture." The nation becomes even more secular as these anti-Christian practices with time become the norm.

Satan has been so successful in confusing the issue of spirituality that I advise that we use biblical references in all our discussions [opinions are useless here]. If the individual (s) does not accept the inerrancy of the Bible there's no argument; because at best the conversation would become opinionated. The writer of Hebrews encourages his readers in their faith through the Word of God, in 4:12 which he states, *"The Word of God is living and powerful, and sharper than any two-edged sword, piercing even to the division of soul and spirit,"* meaning it reveals whether a person is living a soulish or spiritual life.

The body life of the church, not the independent Christian, is the key to understanding God's story in the New Testament. We should not presume that the apostles thought with a predisposition toward rugged individualism. God deals with the church as a body and with individuals as parts or members. Individual members must put the body's concerns above their own. This will open our understanding to the dynamic truth concerning the Christian's godly spirituality which God intended.

In summary, Christian or godly spirituality not only announces the kingdom of God but also seeks to inaugurate the kingdom in the biblical sense. The Christian experience must stress obedience. This call to obedience is a call to forsake the false counterfeits of the culture; which are often identified as personal sins only. It is absolutely true; the Christian is called to flee the personal sins of immorality, impurity, evil desires, greed, anger, strife, malice wrath, lying, and the like. To live these values is to live under the rule of Satan. Often we fail to see the controlling presence of these sins not only in our souls though we have accepted Christ. Through the Word of God and the Holy Spirit, we can be cleansed of these holdovers (sins) in our flesh. To do so our minds must be renewed through the Word of God. Otherwise we miss both the depth in our biblical understanding of sin and also the depth of the kingdom of God as the rule of Christ in every area of daily life. At this point we have gotten our (sins) forgiven, but we have not gotten rid of the factory that produces them, (sin) in the flesh, (soul and body). We are justified by God, but our sanctification and discipleship can be highly hindered by our reluctance to be obedient and die to self; that we might live unto God (see Romans 6:3-4).

REFLECTION

By wisdom a house is built,
and through understanding it is established;
through knowledge its rooms are filled
with rare and beautiful treasures
(Proverbs 24:3-4).

Review Responses (Chapter 6)

1. The most important thing I learned from this chapter was:

2. The area that I need to work on the must to:

3. I can apply this lesson to my life by:

4. Closing statement of Commitment:

CHAPTER 7

DEPLETING YOUR SPIRITUALITY

Then Peter said unto them.
Repent, and be baptized every one of you in the name
of Jesus Christ for the remission of sins, and you shall
receive the gift of the Holy Ghost (Acts 2:38).

Jesus Christ did not begin His ministry until He received a special bestowal of Holy Spirit power. Listen to His words, *"The Spirit of the Lord is upon Me, because He has anointed Me to preach"* (Luke 4:18). Peter summarized Christ's ministry by saying, *"God anointed Jesus of Nazareth with the Holy Spirit and power"* (Acts 10:38). Jesus used the same power in His earthly ministry that we must use *today,* the power of the Spirit. He chose not to minister through His inherent deity, but through the anointing of the Holy Spirit.

The Spirit's power is greatly essential for doing God's work, but it is expended by use. We cannot minister today in yesterday's power. Nor can we accomplish God's full purpose on memories of past blessings and past empowerment. God does not want us trying to live in the past, but in "today" in its moment by moment appropriation of His power.

Spiritual Depletion

Luke 6:19 explains, *"The people all tried to touch Him, because power was coming from Him and healing them all."* This was the power of the Spirit. When the woman who had been suffering for twelve years touched the hem of Jesus' garment, He said, *"Someone touched Me; I know that power has gone out of Me" (Luke 8:46)*. In ministry, if your input is not keeping up with your outflow, at some point you will suffer spiritual depletion. Jesus, our example often rose early or went away alone to be replenished with the power of the Holy Spirit through engaging prayer. What is true of Jesus is true of you. If you are fit to be used of God, His power must be upon you continually (see Ephesians 5:18) and it flows through you in ministry to others.

The Spirit-filled Christian walking in the light of the Word and guided by the Holy Spirit seeks constantly to please God. Moment by moment he or she depends on the Spirit who indwells, and enables you to be victorious over temptation. Through the Spirit's help godly spirituality can be maintained. How?

- By keeping ourselves pure (see 1 Timothy 5:22)
- By careful obedience to the Holy Spirit (1 John 3:3)
- By testing everything, holding on to the good and avoiding the evil (see 1 Thessalonians 5:21-22).
- By keeping ourselves from being spotted by sin (see 1 Peter 3:14)

Have you once known more of the power of God upon you and more of His anointing than you know these days? Keep reading!

Living in a Secular World

We are living in a secular world; and therefore, we live with all kinds of human associations. God never intended for us to be recluses and isolate ourselves from the contaminating influences of life. We are to be salt and light in our world. But if the salt is expended by use and the light is expended by burning, then we are depleting our spirituality. There is no conflict between hard work and spirituality. Certainly there is a correlation between hard work and the best Christian workers and intercessors. Many people forfeit their blessings because they are too lazy to study the Word and to maintain a vibrant prayer life. They let almost anything take priority over spiritual replenishment.

The end of such living finds you trying to succeed by your own power rather than by God's Spirit. The story is told of a little boy who prayed, "Lord if you can't make me a better boy, that's alright I'm having a good time just as I am." While they are slow to speak it many Christians agree with this little boy. Many of these people know nothing of the spiritual secret in the lesson of Zechariah 4, "Not by might, nor by power, but by my Spirit,' says the Lord almighty" (Zechariah 4:6).

If we are to succeed in the secular world, we must reinforce our spirituality with some holy habits. Such reinforcements buttress us against the many activities and environments which are not conducive to spiritual activity, and many of them are anti-spiritual. Living a Christian life as a minister of the gospel in the U.S. Army had its challenges in many forms, sinful jokes, cursing, blaspheming of God's name, rejection in some social circles, even harassing phone calls, just to name a few—*unless you resort constantly to the Lord [KEY!] you will suffer a gradual depletion of your spirituality.*

The glory of living a godly life is it makes you a testimony of God's grace and power. Though I lived many years in Satan's camp, God rescued me in time to make a difference. Praying for my soldiers and living a balanced life before them encouraged them to do the right thing. My outfit had less disciplinary problems and my wife and I became mom and pop for hundreds of soldiers even some young officers. Two of those young company grade officers are now retired Lieutenant Generals.

Nearly three decades have passed [twenty-nine years of pastoral ministry included] since my retirement from the military, and yet by the grace of God my wife and I continue to receive occasional cards, letters, pictures, e-mails, phone calls from these then young people updating us concerning their successes and yes, their failures also. God is good!

Certainly our hearts are encouraged. We should spiritually refresh ourselves with frequent moments in the Lord's presence. I tell you if you continue faithfully; eventually you will become a testimony of God's power and grace to counter present ungodliness. Constant fellowship with the Lord throughout the day certainly develops a godly spirituality. God longs to give His Spirit abundantly to all of His children, and especially those Christians leaders serving in secular settings. Do you hunger and thirst as deeply for the Spirit's power and presence as God hungers to give it to you?

It grieves me greatly to read about and see almost daily the deterioration in the lives of our veterans from the Iraq and Afghanistan wars. Put simply, we had a culture of godly influence to return to when we returned from the two World Wars, Korea, and Vietnam; but our culture today is charged with anti-Christian sentiment in spite of the presence of truth on every hand. The world now has its own cures for every malady including those that are spiritual. The rejection of Christ, Christians, and truth is at an all time high! God forbid!

The Process of Spirituality

God has a destiny for each of His children to fulfill within this lifetime. Therefore, He longs to make covenant with each of us in order to facilitate that destiny. He says, *"For I know the thoughts that I think toward you, says the Lord, thoughts of peace and not of evil, to give you a future and a hope. Then you will call upon Me and go and pray to Me, and I will listen to you. And you will seek Me and find Me, when you search for Me with all your heart" (Jeremiah29:11-13).*

We must discover God's plan for our personal spiritual lives. The way to do that is to listen and be vigilant in our search for Him with all our hearts and obey His commandments. Continue to develop your holy habits; they will help move you along in the process to new levels of spirituality:

- **Submit to God.** To submit is to make a consecrated decision to give myself wholly to God, by simply yielding in obedience to Him, and doing His will (see James 4:7). We must also put on the whole armor of God, an image that includes everything from placing our faith in Christ to our consecrated immersing ourselves in the truths of God's Word (see Ephesians 6:11-18).

- **Resist the devil.** Romans 6:14, says *"For sin shall not have dominion over you, for you are not under law but grace."* Say "NO!" to sin whenever it confronts you. Recognize that you are really free from its demands. Obedience to the Word of God gains a new nature of holiness. Satan will have no choice but to flee, for we belong to the army of the living God.

- **Draw near to God.** Draw near to God when in need. Believe He understands your suffering. Hebrews 4:16 says, *Let us therefore come boldly to the throne of grace, that we may obtain mercy and find grace to help in time of need.* James 4:8 promises, *Draw near to God and He will draw near to you. Cleanse your hands you sinners; and purify your hearts, you double-minded.* Humble yourself before the Lord, and He will lift you up (see James 4:10; 1 Peter 5:6).

- **Gain Revelation.** As the apostle Paul prayed for the Ephesians, I to pray, that the God of our Lord Jesus Christ, the Father of glory may give to you the spirit of wisdom and revelation, meaning to reveal; to manifest;

to unveil; to uncover; to open in the knowledge of Him. It is the work of the Holy Spirit to reveal the knowledge of God to Christians. In fact it is the work of the Spirit to reveal the meaning of all truth to the Christian (see John 14:26; 16:12-15). This is clearly seen in 1 Corinthians 1:9-16 where the wisdom of the world is contrasted with the wisdom of God. Godly spirituality in a Christian sees (through the Spirit's revealing to him or her) the meaning behind world events as well as day to day experiences. He or she understands who and what is behind the events of history and human experience. Therefore, the Christian gains knowledge of God day by day. First, the God that we are to know is the same God that Jesus Christ worshipped when He was on earth as a Man; the God whom Jesus Christ came to *reveal* to mankind. The God we are to know is the Father of glory, that is, the only true and living God. Christians must have an ever increasing knowledge of Him. Three things are essential if we are to grow in the knowledge of Him:

1. To grow in the knowledge of God a Christian must have the *spirit of wisdom;* meaning what we need from God is *a spirit:*

   - That reaches out and grasps after wisdom
   - That hungers and thirsts after wisdom
   - That seeks and seeks after wisdom

2. To grow in the knowledge of God a Christian must have the *spirit of revelation;*

   - A spirit that drives after God
   - A spirit that seeks to know God
   - A spirit that hungers and thirsts after God above all else

3. To grow in the knowledge of God a Christian must:

    •   Have the eyes of his or her heart enlightened.
    •   Have his or her heart open and focus their affection, intelligence, and will upon knowing God
    •   Have the Holy Spirit to enlighten and flood their heart with the things of God

    "For God, who commanded the light to shine out of darkness, hath shined in our hearts, to give the light of the knowledge of the glory of God in the face of Jesus Christ" (2 Corinthians 4:6).

The Results of the Process

We experience the blessings of God and:

•   We should be holy and without blame, living before Him forever and ever in love (v. 4).
•   We should experience what it means to be adopted as children of God forever and ever (vv. 5-6).
•   We should experience eternal redemption and forgiveness of sin (v. 7).
•   We should possess the wisdom and understanding of God (v. 8).

It is not good enough merely to know the truth; we must live it! Simply stated, God has called us to stand before Him in the name and righteousness of Jesus Christ; to stand before Him just as Jesus Christ stands before Him: perfect. It is evident that we are not perfect, not now in what we know as time—but to the Eternal Father those of us who are His, are perfect in His eyes, through Jesus Christ, our Savior and Lord. *"The Spirit itself beareth witness with our spirit, that we are the children of God: and if children, then heirs; heirs of God, and joint-heirs with Christ; if so be that we suffer with him, that we may be also glorified together" (Romans 8:16-17 KJV). Now unto him that is able to do exceeding abundantly above all that we ask or think, according to the power that worketh in us" (Ephesians 3:20).*

REFLECTION

"Now therefore, listen to me my children,
for blessed are those who keep my ways
(Proverbs 8:32).

Study Responses (Chapter 7)

1. The most important things I learned from this chapter was:

2. The area that I need to work on the most is:

3. I can apply this lesson to my life by:

4. Closing statement of Commitment:

SECTION III

VICTORY IN JESUS

CHAPTER 8

THE CHURCH WILL RISE

These people draw near to Me with their mouth, and
honor me with their lips, but their heart is far from Me.
And in vain they worship Me, teaching as doctrines the
commandments of men."
(Matthew 15:8-9)

The depth and breadth of Satan's imbedded attacks and deceptions
in this nation are heating up everywhere substituting institutional
social work rather than a work of grace especially with such
institutional building blocks as government, marriage and the
family. However, the most defying attack is the rejection of Jesus
Christ, His people, and the things of God. For instance, the notion
that any religion is alright as long as Jesus Christ is *not* in it.
Another deception is societal pressures to convince the public
that it is politically incorrect to witness about Jesus or as for as
that matters to mention His name in public. This ruse has even
deceived some Christians. It's so tragic to see politicians, other
public officials, and some church leaders scrambling to settle the
woes of the people knowing that the proper solution is not in the
power of humanity alone; yet, Jesus Christ, the only viable answer
to man's predicament is given little or no consideration.

Signs of the times

In Matthew 24:37-39, Jesus said, *"But as the days of Noah were so will the coming of the Son of Man be. For as in the days before the flood, they were eating and drinking, marrying and giving in marriage, until the day that Noah entered the ark, and did not know until the flood came and took them all away, so also will the coming of the Son of man be."* As a PK, preacher's kid, growing up, I heard this passage elaborated on many times. Most people then put much emphasis on the vices of drinking and riotous living, etc. However for today's illumination of this passage by the Spirit, we see that Jesus was referring to the indifference of the people of that time to the coming disaster. There is nothing sinful about eating and non-intoxicating drinking, marrying and giving in marriage. However, the people of the end times will be doing the same things with the feeling of accountability to no one. Our society has become less influenced by the Gospel; and there is little thought for the fear of God or the coming judgment.

In (vv. 4-14) Jesus gave the disciples a warning against false signs that we should concern ourselves with today since these signs and activities of our times are so similar. He sketched the prevailing conditions of their present age down to the very end. There will be religious deception, social and political upheavals everywhere, natural calamities, disloyalty, and persecution, all of which are signs of the end times. In verse 13, I see the church without spot, *("He who endures!")*. Verse 14 assures us that in spite of the difficulties in the midst we are to persevere in preaching the gospel of the kingdom everywhere.

Many postmodern churches have been secularized and try to proclaim the gospel through song (hip-hop gospel and jazz gospel etc.), dance and so-called gospel plays to name a few. These substitutes draw far larger crowds than the lone godly spirituality proclaiming the true gospel of Christ by word of mouth, deed, and true Christian witness in the grocery stores, on the job, in the home, schools, jails, rest homes, hospitals, highways and by-ways.

Many times when it seems no one is listening, the anointed Word of God saves, delivers, break yokes, and bring down strongholds.

It's time to leave behind the old "I heard," and the "courts of personal, popular, and public opinions." One of the major considerations in any battle is to insure that your forces, weaponry and necessary support equipment are tailored for the specific mission at hand. Carry only the necessities and leave the rest behind. The church today seems to be trying to fight the battle with programs and goals (excess baggage) established by their founders many years ago. Many of the functions the churches are struggling with today were established as means to specific ends. Again, I refer to Special Days (fundraisers) which for the most part have taken over the church calendar. Many of our students complain of how little concern there is for the lack of proper biblical teaching and training in their churches. However, over the years the means have become ends, and the very purpose for their establishment has long been forgotten. In many churches, this humdrum of "same old same old" has created an atmosphere of unbelief which makes it difficult for them to distinguish a true godly spirituality from their familiar ungodly one. The world around us is changing at an unprecedented pace. Much of what worked a decade ago is already obsolete. Social analysts estimate that our culture *reinvents* itself every three to five years; that is actually two years earlier than the five to seven years of my generation's teaching.

It's very challenging for the innovative young men and women who are heeding the call to the *gospel* ministry today. Many are leaving the traditional churches because of the leadership's denial of these cataclysmic changes in the culture around them. Therefore their responses if any at all to the changes make little or no difference. In their frustration, many are returning to the store front and house church models of doing church while hearing the words of Jesus, "Where two or three are gathered in My name I will be in the midst." As a teacher I am often confronted with the question, "Why are all of these little churches popping up all over the place?" The individual will then proceed to give his or her own answer, "We only need one church!" That too is a deceptive answer.

While serving in the military around the world, my wife and I were often attracted to the non-traditional churches, with a missions-flavor, because their focus always seemed to be the furtherance and preaching of "the gospel to every creature" (see Mark 16:15). Additionally, they established a climate of faith for healing the whole person; through the promotion of a personal knowledge and saving experience with Jesus Christ. My family grew in the knowledge of our Savior!

Upon retiring from the military, I completed Bible College and went into the pastorate of denominational churches. Right a way I began to have conflicts popup between denominational traditions, teaching, doctrine and Biblical truth. There seemed to be a book some where that someone had written to cover every subject; much of it their personal theology. Very little problem solving is done using the Bible therefore, forging a truly biblical worldview is not a priority. Certainly this carelessness is reflected in the lack of a harvest in a great number of our communities. Notice the newspapers' crime page in any city U.S.A. In 1998 my wife and I founded the Bread of Life Bible Institute, a non-traditional institution for the equipping of the saints to do the work of ministry [more on that in a later chapter].

One of our major tasks is to help build a biblical worldview in each student. Many people inquire why we are non-traditional and non-accredited. The answer, our focus is geared to "what you are" (before) "what you do." The focus of our curriculum does not allow the traditional systematic methodology, in order to be flexible in meeting the needs of the present hour. Our student body is comprised of professionals and non-professionals. We have those possessing graduate degrees and those with GED certificates. We have some who are of the retirement age and others just starting out in their Christian life or ministry. All with one focus, biblical revelation truth, Jesus Christ!

A couple of years into this ministry, we detected a very serious vacuum in the local churches due to a lack of biblical teaching and training with an extraordinary dependence on the Sunday sermon to fill the void. This impossible task that many pastors have taken on has caused many Christians to leave the church in frustration and others who never joined a church [claiming they aren't being fed]. Both are starving from a deficiency of biblical truth. As a result, we began establishing non-traditional Bible schools and planting and fellowshipping with churches followed. Word of mouth has always been our advertisement. Some of the fellowship churches began birthing other Bible-based churches and ministries.

Perhaps you are concluding that I am against the denominational church, far from it. I do not presently belong to a denomination, yet I have a great deal of respect for them. We independent ministries can learn much from mainline Christian denominations. They have creeds, church history, a system of ordination, ministry placement and criteria for ministry training. They have successes and failures, so we can be eclectic profiting from their strengths and avoiding their weaknesses. Let's not forget we all [Christian churches] draw our beginning from the early apostolic church. They have an understanding of culture, theology and involve themselves with public policy issues. Most of our students belong to them. Our cadre including my wife and I came from denominational backgrounds. However, all Christians need a truly biblical worldview to counter the ungodly spirituality raging in this nation. Both denominational and independent apostolic congregations often lose their children to the world because the media present a sophisticated humanistic worldview. We aren't effectively teaching the next generation according to Deuteronomy 6:6-8 as we should be. We must prioritize a more meaningful relationship with Christ and deeper knowledge through the teaching of the truths of God's Word. We need to demonstrate through word and godly spirituality the kingdom of God on the earth. This spiritual ignorance in our children produces an environment conducive to deceptive and rebellious nature in them that leaves them open to the influences of anti-Christian mind-sets. For a deeper study see my books *["How Should We then Live," and "Behold the Man"]*.

I ran into problems as a pastor trying to change even the names of some of the church's organizations activities hoping to provide a broader focus on holistic ministry. For instance BTU (Baptist Training Union) to CTU (Christian Training Union), the idea being to get away from the program model and back to maturity through building a biblical worldview based on the Holy Spirit and the truth of God's Word. This nation has moved from a Judeo-Christian community to a global community of multi-cultural religions. Different cultural beliefs and influences are being blurred among our youth because of the promotion of multiculturalism. I take anything with a lone "ism" on it as another potential religion. So no matter what it is—our focus should be to faithfully and truthfully endure at living, proclaiming and spreading the gospel of the kingdom, Jesus Christ.

It was accounted to Francis of Assisi to have said of the Gospel, "preach, preach and sometimes use words!" Like the apostle Paul in 2 Corinthians 12:9, his desire was for more of the abiding power of Christ communicating through him. Christ has promised power when the Holy Spirit comes upon His children (see Acts 1:8). We should also want to live day by day within the atmosphere of His power as a living testimony. It may seem like the church has been overwhelmed by the god of this world and his forces, but in reality the true church continues to march forward and upward [see my book "The Blood Runs Through"].

Made perfect in weakness

During my early years in military leadership I experienced an event one day that changed my way of doing and thinking about many things concerning my Christian walk. One morning as I was getting out of my car at work, I noticed a sedan sitting outside of my office entrance. The occupant was a man higher in my chain of command who truly disliked me because I was a Christian. I groaned and remarked to myself, I thought, "O Lord, not this morning!" I was overheard by one of my *unsaved* coworkers; who walked up close to me laughed and said, "I bet he makes you pray." Lesson #1, don't try to face the opposition in your own strength and #2 don't let the world make you sweat, they love it!

After that little incident in the parking lot I came under conviction, confessed, repented and asked the Lord's forgiveness, then I went on to my office and watched the man's wrath melt down to a frustrated conversation. A few days later, he suffered a heart attack. You guessed it! The Spirit spoke to me to go and visit him in the hospital. I reluctantly went on. This man lying on that bed was nothing of the Goliath I dreaded to see coming my way. Yep, I had to pray with him. Later after his recovery, he came by to see me and thank me for the hospital visit; and to inform me that he had been reassigned to another duty station. Here stood my defeated Goliath. The Lord came to my rescue. Weakness does not create power; *but weakness drives us to God, the Source of divine power.* That principle holds true personally and corporately. Periodically my mind briefly visits that encounter through flash backs.

When through revelation Paul recognized that his thorn in the flesh (v. 7), along with all other opposition, dangers, and sufferings during his years of all-out witness for Christ (see 2 Corinthians 11:23-30) served to drive him closer to God and to constant dependence on Him, listen to his response, *"That is why for Christ's sake, I delight in weaknesses, in insults, in hardships, in persecutions, in difficulties. For when I am weak, then I am strong"* (2 Corinthians 12:10).

When we recognize how weak and insufficient we are, we should call on God, cling to Him, and make this verse the constant cry of our hearts. What have you experienced of this holy power? Filled with that power, energized by that power, clothed in that power, endued for your ministry of reconciliation by that power which is Christ Himself (see 1 Corinthians 1:24) manifest through the Holy Spirit (see 1 Peter 1:11; Acts 1:8).

As He ascended, Jesus promised that power to us; and it is available today for our task of evangelism, taking the gospel to the ends of the earth. Christ commands us to tell others about Him regardless of the prevailing conditions and circumstances. We are told that all but one of the eleven that heard this promise became martyrs (John died in exile). God empowered His disciples to be faithful witnesses even when they were facing the most trying opposition and even certain death. Jesus promised that He would not leave nor forsake us, but would be with us always even to the end of the age (see Matthew 28:20; John 14:18). He fulfilled the promise in the coming of the Holy Spirit, who dwells within true Christians (see John 16:4-7). Christianity is a life (Christ) and a lifestyle (godly spirituality).

I believe that there are some dangerous days ahead for Christians in the local churches where many pastors like the disciples who've gone on before will face persecution and even death; as we wait for our Lord. Many of the church members are scattering because the pastors for whatever reason fail to study properly or see the need for their own spiritual empowerment. While changes in the culture do not change the gospel of Christ, it certainly should cause us to change our methodology, terminology and up close help our ability to see reality. In this present day many Christians are going into the closet because they are afraid to face even the mildest persecution. At the same time immorality in all forms has come out of the closet. We had better settle truly whose side we're on! Recently in our city, an eleven year old boy leaving a Quick Stop Store on his bicycle was held up in the parking lot and robbed at gunpoint by a grown man (the child reportedly had two dollars!).

The airways are filled with politicians talking about creating more jobs, fixing the economy, how they can improve foreign policy, and how if they win the office—they will do this and that to fix all. Any individual possessing that much ability should be able to influence for the good of the people without being president or holding any public office.

Oh! How refreshing it would be for just one of them to sincerely acknowledge God publicly in their discourse. Just siding with a certain faith or religion for the vote is not going to help anymore than a man sleeping overnight in a garage; and then running out into heavy traffic the next morning crying, "I'm a car, I'm a car simply because he slept in the garage all night!" Both are tragedies! Christ said, *"I am the vine, you are the branches, He who abides in Me, and I in him, bears much fruit; for without Me you can do nothing" (John 15:5).* For the branch to produce more fruit, it must abide, which means to dwell, to stay, to settle in permanently, and to sink deeper. The way the child of God abides in Christ is to faithfully obey Him (see 15:10; 1 John 3:24). The Christian who lovingly obeys the Word of God produces much fruit.

Christ is coming

Among the most comforting words in all Scripture; from Jesus' own lips, *"Let not your heart be troubled; you believe in God believe also in Me. In My Father's house are many mansions; if it were not so, I would have told you. I go to prepare a place for you. And if I go and prepare a place for you, I will come again and receive you to Myself; that where I am, there you may be also" (see John 14:1-3).* We have the personal promise that Jesus is returning for us. Just think of that! His personal signature is on our salvation; as we have received Him. He spoke these words to His disciples during the most intimate time; and they continue to echo down through the ages to us, the bride of Christ as a precious promise. *"And everyone who has this hope in Him purifies himself, just as He is **pure**" (1 John 3:3).* The very prospect of being transformed into the likeness of Christ should motivate all Christians to live righteously; *we are the children of God!* Regeneration (see John 3:3) is an experience the **world** cannot understand (see 1 John 3:1-2).

Our faith is based on knowledge of God's Word and His Character. The spirit of this world (Satan) is in opposition to God. He knows when we **determine to stand in faith** with Christ as our object, (**godly spirituality**); the world loses control and its non-spiritual influence over us. Christ is coming to receive us; and we look forward to that day in expectation, *"making ourselves ready!"*

When the coming of Christ is preached or taught among some church folks; the group quickly divides into two groups: One group is ready and resting in a sense of comfort and anticipation. While the other is not ready for His coming; and are in denial and unbelief displaying a mixture of responses:

- Some are irritated.
- Some are intimidated.
- Some are afraid even a little panicked.
- Some simply *refuse* to think about it.

But in reality no one can remain neutral on the subject. The teaching of prophecy has a tendency of sending some people into an exciting orbit; while others are driven away. I have always loved the study of prophecy beginning back in my Bible school days. Through the years I have enjoyed and used the urgency of the hour, wisdom and insight the Spirit has imparted in ministry; but at the same time maintaining a practical equilibrium with the here and now.

A few months ago the entire world shared in the failure of one preacher who tried to set a date on Christ's return for His bride, the church. It didn't happen so he adjusted his date; and that date failed to materialize also. In years past I'm sure that many of us would have read about this type incident in the newspaper or heard about it and eventually just shrugged it off. However, this time the media frenzy really revealed the destructive power of such fanaticism. Some people had resigned from their jobs, others reportedly gave away their life savings and material goods, but it didn't happen! So, the real tragedy occurred when these people tried to return to their jobs or other pieces of the lives they had given up; just to find rejection, laughter, and ridicule. Was God glorified in this? I heard a preacher say, "at least many people worldwide heard about the day of reckoning; which is sure to come!"

The enemy loves to say, "I told you so!" A few days ago another world-known preacher leaked to the media, that God had given him the name of the next person to be elected president of the United States. Why would he in particular need to know that? From what I was able to find out, he did not call a name. Thank God! Las Vegas and other world centers of gambling would have been handed a free field day (for taking bets).

However, these incidents just reinforce excuses to ignore biblical truth; and thereby deny the blessed hope, comfort, encouragement, spiritual growth, and stability found in true biblically-based prophecy. The flipsides of that are those who through ignorance and unbelief don't believe it's going to happen; so they simply become more insensitive. The sad outcome of such ungodliness is the widening of the gap between the two spiritualities, (godly and ungodly). People hear the truth through preaching, teaching and witnessing, yet they seem to have acquired a "built-in immunity" against biblical truth!

Oh! But God is real! In contrast to the examples above, a couple of days ago ABC evening news aired an actual live testimony. A pastor was on his way to closeout the paperwork and foreclosure of his church, when an anonymous individual approached him and informed that he had heard of their plight. He then asked the pastor how much was owed on the mortgage, the pastor replied, $325, 000. The donor paid the bill in full. A newsman asked the pastor for a comment, he replied, "we prayed!" The camera shifted away from the pastor, but not before the glory of the Lord was displayed.

My last conversation with Mother

My last conversation with my 96 year old godly mother was on the subject of the rapture. I shared with her one of my frustrations, as a pastor in that, "I find myself disturbed as the older saints die, many of those entering the church to replace them are having acute problems with their spirituality." And I concluded my illustrious comments with something like, "The Lord had better hurry with the rapture or there will be no spiritually mature saints left in many of the churches!" She looked straight into my eyes and said, "Son, how do you know the rapture isn't already taking place?" As if to say, watch that systematic theology. She passed into the Lord's presence that night. She was not sick, not on medication, still drove her car to church, the store for her groceries, and worked her own good sized garden. My comfort came in reading 2 Corinthians 5:8, which my wife and I drew from for her epitaph, *"We are confident, yes, well pleased rather to be absent from the body and to be present with the Lord."* Amen. When we live well—we die well!

A few days ago I took part in the burial of a good friend and brother in the Lord. He was a Veteran of World War II, Joshua Brown, who served faithfully as Chairman of the Board of Trustees in the church of which I was pastor. He acted as superintendent in the construction of the new church facilities; I could not get to the construction site before him nor have information about the work that he was not aware of. He was always there! He was faithful and dedicated to the Lord's work. As always during these services my thoughts of Jesus' return came to my mind as in 1 Thessalonians 4:16-17:

> *For the Lord Himself will descend from heaven with*
> *a shout, with the voice of an archangel, and with the*
> *trumpet of God. And the dead in Christ will rise first.*
> *Then we who are alive and remain shall be **caught up***
> *together with them in the clouds to meet the Lord in*
> *the air and thus we shall always be with the Lord.*

Whether young or old, those who pass into eternity have the same truth to claim as we who remain. That promise is something to wrap your heart around, especially when it seems that all hell has broken loose in your life. At times when the events of your day seem out of control for no known reason; think on these things and be reminded that the end is not yet. God has given us the truth concerning His Son's return to encourage the saints no matter the circumstances. Take a quick look, right at the end of that great resurrection chapter, 1 Corinthians 15 and verse 58, concerning Jesus' return and exhorting us to stay at the tasks of faithful and righteous living, so that we will be ready.

He can return at any moment; and certainly we do not desire to be embarrassed in meeting Him face to face: *Therefore, my beloved brethren, be steadfast, immovable, always abounding in the work of the Lord, knowing that your labor is not in vain in Lord.* Never give up! Continue steadfastly in the faith of *Jude 3,* and abound in your service to God.

REFLECTION

"Now therefore, listen to me, my children;
Pay attention to the words of my mouth:
Do not let your heart turn aside to her ways"
(Proverbs 7:24-25)

Study Questions (Chapter 8)

1. The most important thing I learned from this chapter was:

2. The area that I need to work on the most is:

3. I can apply this lesson to my life by:

4. Closing statement of Commitment:

CHAPTER 9

A HOLY COMMUNITY

*"I therefore, a prisoner for the Lord, beg you to lead
a life worthy of the calling to which you have been
called, with all lowliness and meekness, with patience,
forbearing one another in love, eager to maintain the
unity of the Spirit in the bond of peace"*
(Ephesians 4:1-3).

The question is often asked, "What is the church to do while waiting for Christ's return?" Luke 19:13 assures us that Jesus expects those who are His (the true church) to "Do business till He comes;" which means we are to *love and serve God faithfully,* as individual Christians and corporately as the church until He appears. Christians should live consecrated lives daily [a godly spirituality] ever mindful that He can appear at any moment. The goal of any viable local church should be to obediently keep unity (oneness) in focus. I think of this oneness like snowflakes each one of them is different from the others; however, when they are molded into a snowball they become one indistinguishable and indivisible. Christ is our King-Priest; therefore, individualism must submit to community. The apostle Peter exhorts, *"But you are a chosen generation, a royal priesthood, a holy nation, His own special people, that you may proclaim the praises of Him who*

called you out of darkness into His marvelous light" (1 Peter 2:9).
This verse provides a direct contrast to the previous stumbling of
individualism, and ungodly spirituality in chapter 8. Here Peter
explains, *"They stumble being disobedient to the Word of God to
which they were called.*

The Holy Spirit and Christ

According to the New Testament, the hopes of God's Old
Testament saints were fulfilled in Jesus Christ. He is the Anointed
One endowed by the Holy Spirit and referenced by the prophets.
The New Testament emphasizes the importance of the Holy Spirit
in Jesus' life:

- The Spirit was responsible for Jesus' conception (Luke
  1:35).
- The Spirit endowed Jesus for His divinely given mission at
  His baptism (Matthew 3:113-15).
- The Spirit guided our Lord's steps from His conception to
  His resurrection (see Matthew 4:1; 12:28).

Jesus Himself promised that He would give His disciples the
full measure of the Spirit, who would be a well of living water
flowing from their inner being (see John 4:14; 7:37-39). As He
departed, Jesus assured His followers that His Father would send
another Counselor like Him, the Holy Spirit, who would not walk
with them but *in* them:

- To empower them for their mission (see John 14:16; 16:1).
- To teach them, reminding them of all the Lord's instructions
  (see John 14:25-27)
- To lead them into truth (see John 16:12-15).
- To testify about Jesus to the world (see John 16:7-11).
- To assist the disciples in taking a stand as Christ's witnesses
  (see John 15:26-27).

The Holy Spirit and the Church

This glorious promise was fulfilled at Pentecost. Pentecost was one of three major Jewish holy days. The Greek word means "fifty," so named because it came on the fiftieth day following the Sabbath of Passover. It was also known as "the Feast of Weeks," "the Firstfruits of the Harvest" and "the Day of the Firstfruits." During this harvest celebration, the Jews brought to God the firstfruits of their harvest in thanksgiving, expecting that God would give the rest of the harvest as His blessing.

This particular Day of Pentecost was the Day of firstfruits of Christ's Church (see Acts 2), *the beginning of the great harvest of souls* through the work of the *Holy Spirit*. Luke records, *"When the Day of Pentecost was fully come, they were all with one accord in one place, and suddenly there came a sound from heaven, as of a rushing mighty wind, and it filled the whole house where they were sitting. Then there appeared to them divided tongues, as of fire, and one sat upon each of them. And they were all filled with the Holy Spirit and began to speak with other tongues, as the Spirit gave them utterance" (Acts 2:1-4).* And there were dwelling in Jerusalem Jews, devout men from every nation under heaven. And when this sound occurred the multitude came together, and were confused, because everyone heard them speak in his own language (see Acts 2:5-6).

The outpouring of the Spirit signaled **the birth of the Spirit-filled, Spirit-empowered, Spirit-led community (the church)!** This event marked a milestone in the history of God's plan (story) in the salvation of humankind. At Pentecost the Holy Spirit entered the world in a unique way; inaugurating a new age, the age of grace, the church age, the age of fulfillment (see 1 Peter 1:10-12).

Beginning with Pentecost the Spirit took on a new role; therefore throughout the age, the Holy Spirit would focus His work on the new community, the fellowship of the followers of Christ. The *reality of Pentecost* was not limited to the disciples. Rather, Pentecost embraces all believers. It extends to every Christian in every nation and in every generation! We all now enjoy the presence of the Holy Spirit, who forms us into one community. 1 Corinthians 12:13 says, *"For by one Spirit we were all baptized into one body—whether Jews or Greeks, whether slaves or free—and have been made to drink into one Spirit."* All believers are baptized into the body of Christ (see Romans 6:3). The Spirit not only surrounds us, He also dwells within us as a "down payment" guaranteeing our future salvation (see 2 Corinthians 1:22; 5:5; Ephesians 1:13-14). We are a work in progress as He has already begun His transforming work within us (see Romans 8:10; 2 Corinthians 3:18). Praise God!

> **Appropriate the power of God's Spirit which**
> **is in you through your union with Christ.**

How? In Christ we are no longer under the sentence of the law, but empowered by the Holy Spirit who *quickened (made alive) our dead spirit in regeneration* to live for Christ and walk according to the Spirit; which is synonymous with being led by the Spirit (see Romans 8:1), "be constantly filled with the Spirit" (Ephesians 5:18).

If we would be the community that our Lord desires us to be, we must grasp a clear understanding of just what this community—the church is. We often talk about the church as if it were simply a building. "My church is at 624 Columbus Apparel Road." Then we equate "church" with "worship service." Are you going to church tomorrow?" Or, "what are you doing after church?" Is it a club or society in which we hold membership?" Is this the church?

NO! None of these usages tell us what the church is. Since the church is an eternal entity in God's story, we must ask the question from a biblical perspective. Who are these relational people? The Holy Spirit is forming them into a community. They are living in fellowship with God, and each other. These people have been *"called out ones"* [out of the world] by the proclamation of the gospel for the express purpose of belonging to God through Christ: "God's nation" *[from every kindred]* a 'holy priesthood" *[shared by all]* who belongs to God (see 1 Peter 2:9; Revelation 5:9). Brackets are mine.

Then the church is spoken of as the body of Christ (see 1 Corinthians 12:27; Ephesians 1:22-23; Colossians 1:18). Like the human body, the church is a unity made up of different parts or members (see 1 Corinthians 12:1-31). Not all members have the same task to fulfill. But all have the same goal; all are concerned for one another and use their gifts in the service of the *whole*. Using the New Testament as a guide leads us to see the church as a local congregation of believers in fellowship together with the purpose of walking together under Christ to be a people-in-relationship, under God's authority and empowered by the Holy Spirit. Together we are to carry on Christ's own ministry and be His physical presence on earth.

Satan seeks to destroy that unity by embedding his decoys within the congregations to cause division and strife. However, the Holy Spirit works through Spirit-filled, gifted individuals enabling them to maintain unity within diversity. Paul speaks of a diversity of spiritual gifts but the same Spirit, and different ministries but the same Lord, and diversities of activities but the same God who works all in all; but the manifestation of the Spirit is given to each one for the profit of all (see 1 Corinthians 12:1-7).

Walk in unity

When Christians through the empowerment of spiritual gifts given by the Holy Spirit consistently *refuse* to accuse and reject one another, choosing instead to forgive and to love one another, strife is replaced by the *unity of the Spirit*. All true Christians are one in the Spirit; and it is our individual and corporate duty to keep that unity, recognize it as real and vigorously maintain it. The Scripture says, *"For as the body is one and has many members, but all the members of that one body, being many, are one body, so also is Christ. For by one Spirit we were all baptized into one body—whether Jews or Greeks, whether slaves or free—and have*

all been made to drink into one Spirit" (1 Corinthians 12:12-13).
Here Paul, the apostle, in comparing the church to a human body,
shows how the wide diversity of gifts *assures* unity in the church.
Each gift contributes something necessary to the common life and
growth of the whole; without any division (see John 17:20-27).
Thus, the church has the power of the Holy Spirit to accomplish
its mission. I stated earlier, Satan has placed his deceiving decoys
within the congregation to cause division and disruptions. A
church or individual in the natural would not stand a chance;
however, we are supernatural. *"For greater is He that is in you,
than he that is in the world" (see 1 John 4:4).*

In Ephesians 4:11-15, the apostle Paul taught that Christ gave
some to be apostles, some prophets, evangelists, some pastors and
teachers, with the threefold purpose of equipping of the saints:

- To do the work of **ministry**.
- To edify or build up of the **body** of Christ.
- To reach the **goal** of maturity, truth, and love.

Church history reflects that from approximately 450 A.D.-
1550 A.D. the Roman Catholic Church was the main depository
of Christianity. The apostolic ministry of Pentecost was replaced
by a religious system of men designated by the Roman church
as priests, bishops, cardinals, and eventually popes. This caused
a bump in the road, but did not stop the work of our Lord in
building His church (see Matthew 16:18).

Through various movements beginning with the Reformation
which began in 1517; the Holy Spirit has been restoring the
Ephesians 4:11 [body] gifts that the Roman system had removed.
Though the way seemed dark during that period, be it known
that at no time since the birth of His church, Pentecost, has there
not been a true blood-washed church [His invisible body] within
visible Christendom without spot. Every since the church's birth at
Pentecost there has been children of God at the "ready to rapture"
upon His appearance!

Shake-down time

Periodically, institutions such as the military, manufacturers, governments and other major corporations schedule periodic shutdowns of various operations and conduct shake-down inspections. They take a look at their operational procedures, size and effectiveness in accomplishing their mission. This is also a time to trim access baggage. In the church this would include evaluation and adjustment of those man-made traditions, customs, cultural issues, and practices of the church that hinder the saints individually and corporately from truly moving forward in their spiritual lives and kingdom service. We have a great insightful advantage over the world in this work. During my years in the military, it was always wise to inspect all new regulations, manuals and directives before implementing them to insure that there were no pending changes that had not been posted to the documents. Actually they came with some changes noted during production.

Our kingdom operations manual, the Holy Bible, written by men under the inspiration of the Holy Spirit more than two thousand years ago has never been changed nor has it ever needed to be changed. It is still the inspired Word of God intact! That truth has through the ages survived the attacks of the devil and the very gates of hell. It remains the only resource for a godly spirituality. It is the faith of Jude 3 [body of truth, the Bible] that the writer continues to admonish the saints to contend for. The same faith and trust in Christ required for Peter's walk on the water, the lady's healing of the issue of blood, the woman's eyes opened at the well; and those heroes of Hebrews 11. All yet serve as examples for us; because true spirituality has not changed. The process remains the same today as then, it all begins with repentance and the new birth, (see John 3:3; also see my book "The Blood Runs Through" for a deeper study).

Jesus laid out for us His plan for His church without spot in the greatest sermon ever preached, the Sermon on the Mount (see Matthew 5-7). He set the standard for what every believer is (**to be**) and (**to do**); not for leaders only. Additionally, He set the example for living the kingdom spirituality Himself! The first observerable standard that He set was to put the Father first in everything. How wonderful it would be if our national and local leaders would honor Him at the beginning of their decision-making processes and acknowledge Him publicly.

In Matthew 5:3-11, Jesus spelled out the character traits by which we are *to be* identified as true Christians displaying true spirituality. Jesus began each of the Beatitudes with "blessed" a word that expresses the happiness, joy, grace, and gratitude of being saved (born again)! He included the following: 1) a pronouncement of blessing. 2) a description of the ones considered to be blessed and 3) an explanation for the blessing:

- Blessed are the poor in spirit, for *theirs is the kingdom of heaven*—those who recognize their spiritual poverty and realize total dependence on God (see v. 3).

- Blessed are those who mourn, for *they shall be comforted*—those who experience the sorrow of true repentance (see v. 4).

- Blessed are the meek, for *they shall inherit the earth*—those who display humility and self-discipline (see v. 5).

- Blessed are they which hunger and thirst after righteousness, for *they shall be filled*—those whose lives have a positive effect by living responsibly to the glory of God (v. 6).

- Blessed are the merciful, for *they shall obtain mercy*—those who display an outlet of mercy (v. 7).

- Blessed are the pure in heart, for *they shall see God*—those who are blood-washed, and undefiled (v. 8).

- Blessed are the peacemakers, for *they shall be the sons of God*—those who follow Christ's example (v. 9).

- Blessed are they who are persecuted for righteousness sake, for *theirs is the kingdom of heaven*—those who suffer because of their loyalty to godly spirituality [righteous living] (v. 10).

- Blessed are you when men shall revile you, and persecute you, and shall say any manner of evil against you falsely, for my sake. *Rejoice and be exceedingly glad, for great is your reward in heaven, for so they persecuted the prophets who were before you*—those who suffer persecution for righteousness sake *(vv. 11, 12)*.

The Beatitudes describe what we are to be as kingdom citizens; and in verses 13-16, Jesus uses the metaphors of salt and light to indicate the kingdom citizen's **influence** for good as they penetrate and circulate secular society. As Christians, we realize that our citizenship is in heaven and we are different—it is that difference that defines us for good. As the salt of the earth, we should make life more palatable for those around us; and as light we should be as moons to the glory of God reflecting His Son wherever we are. Our character traits (what we are!) determines our influence in (what we do!). The devil is spreading a false spirituality trying to counter our true spirituality, but Christ warned us to be suspect of things that are popular or favored by the worldly-minded majority. *"Beware of false prophets, who come to you in sheep's clothing, but inwardly they are ravenous wolves.* He went on to explain, *"You will know them by their fruits. Do men gather grapes from thornbushes or figs from thistles? Even so, every good tree bears good fruit, but a bad tree bears bad fruit." (vv. 16-18).*

Jesus motivates those who are His to live righteously by emphasizing that such living is the result of the new nature; which came with love and trust; and not through observance of some societal code of ethics. There is a marked difference between a correct behavior, based only on the Law, and righteous actions that proceed from the new nature acquired through the new birth in Christ (see 2 Corinthians 5:17; John 3:3 also see Galatians 5:22-23).

REFLECTION

But the path of the just is like the shining sun,
That shines ever brighter unto the perfect day
(Proverbs 4:18).

Review Responses (Chapter 9)

1. The most important thing I learned from this chapter was:

2. The area that I need to work on the most is:

3. I can apply this lesson to my life by:

4. Closing statement of Commitment:

CHAPTER 10

COMMUNITY (CHURCH) ORIDNANCES

"If when we were enemies we were reconciled to God through the death of His Son, much more, having been reconciled, we shall be saved by His life"
(Romans 5:10).

The church is a special people who glorify God by walking together as a community, thereby reflecting the character of the Triune God, who is love. Church membership is not joining a club or fraternity however, it means participating in a body of people who share God's story, a vision, and a mandate to live in the pattern of the *death* and *resurrection* of Jesus Christ. True godly spirituality for the Christian is to identify with Him in His death and resurrection. The process of entering the church involves sealing a "covenant" (a mutual agreement) with born again, like-minded, like-committed persons in a specific location to walk together as Jesus' disciples, incorporated into a community. All communities engage in certain symbolic acts that represent their life together. As Christians two practices are especially significant [*baptism* and *the Lord's Supper*], which is also known as communion. These two ordinances become the community's "acts of commitment."

Acts of Commitment

Throughout the church age, Christians have participated in these acts (ordinances). Yet there remains much confusion and disagreement concerning baptism and the Lord's Supper. An "ordinance" is an act which Christ ordained and, therefore, we practice as a sign of our obedience to Him. He gave them to the church as a means for us:

- To declare our loyalty to Him.
- To confess our faith in a special manner.
- To present a picture of God's grace given in Christ.
- To participate in announcing the gospel and bearing testimony by our obedient response to the good news.
- To participate in the reality the acts symbolize.
- To right standing with God only as we are likewise being brought into right relationship with others.

The Apostle Paul's significant contribution on godly spirituality is in his discussion of baptism in Romans 6:4, *"Therefore we were **buried** with Him through **baptism** into **death,** that just as Christ was **raised from the dead** by the glory of the Father, even so we should **walk in newness of life."** Jesus' death becomes our death. Christian baptism makes these spiritual realities manifest for all to see.

Newness of Life (Baptism)

If the Christian's identification with Christ means being identified with His death, then it logically follows that the Christian also identifies with Jesus' resurrection. Having died and now having been raised with Christ, the Christian should live a different kind of life. Newness of life is the result of our no longer being connected to the sin nature of Adam. The **old man** was crucified with Christ (see Galatians 2:20). Simply put, the born again Christian is not the same person he or she was before conversion. The Christian is a new creation. *"Therefore, if anyone is in Christ, he is a new creation; old things have passed away; behold all things have become new" (2 Corinthians 5:17).* Remember, we walk by faith not by sight. Paul is presenting the results of Christ's death for the believer and the believer's death with Him (see 1 Corinthians 5:14). Because Christians are united with Jesus both in His death and resurrection, they participate in the new creation. That is, they receive the benefits of being *restored* by Christ to what God had originally created them to be (see Genesis 1:26; 1 Corinthians 15:45-49). A Christian's life should change, because he or she is being transformed into the likeness of Christ (3:18). Instead of evaluating others with the values of the world [the five senses] a Christian looks at the world through the eyes of faith, beyond the natural (v. 16).

The Christian is no longer enslaved to the old sinful nature; nor obligated to sin. As Christians, we must know that we have **died to sin** (see Romans 6:6-8) and have been **made alive with Christ,** we must believe this! In our identity with the death and resurrection of Jesus, we live a life empowered by the Holy Spirit, a life that continually dies and rises to the life of the Spirit.

It is in vogue today in many churches to downgrade and even neglect baptism in favor of decisional faith, to the point of baptizing immediately following the particular service in which the convert first believed. This is kind of like giving a diploma to the student at the beginning of a course of study. The early church fathers associated faith and baptism together, but they placed a greater emphasis on the ordinance of baptism than many churches do today.

A great analogy is that of engagement and marriage. While the ceremony affirms the love and commitment of the couple being married, it also confers upon that couple new rights and responsibilities. In the same way baptism confirms the faith already acknowledged by the convert and symbolizes the new relationship with God and calls the newly baptized into a new life of living out his or her new relationship with Christ and others. It is faith in

Christ and a baptism into His death and resurrection that images the meaning of true godly spirituality.

Because a person trusts in Christ and has signified this faith through baptism, his or her calling in faith and baptism is to live a life in the face of evil that always shines. For as long as that wicked enemy of our souls, sees the shining of our spiritual robe, he will not dare come near, because he is so afraid of its brightness (blinds his eyes).

In summary, godly spirituality is rooted in our identification with the death and resurrection of Jesus, and the call to live in the pattern of death to the old and a resurrection to the new must be preached and witnessed. Our preaching should call people to live their baptism; because here is an image that will catch the imagination of the people of post Christian thought and sow a seed that will take a lifetime to harvest!

The Lord's Supper

The same kind of confusion and disagreement comes up concerning the Lord's Supper, our second ordinance. In the early church and probably in most Protestant churches in America today communion is celebrated on the first Sunday of the month. Some churches celebrate once a quarter. Today we are rediscovering the power of symbolic communication and rethinking the teachings of Scripture on the meaning of the Lord's Supper. Consequently many churches are increasing the frequency of the celebration; some from quarterly to monthly, others from monthly to biweekly, and a few to weekly. Other names for this ordinance are the Eucharist, and the breaking of bread.

Many people in our churches know very little about the meaning of the Communion because there is so little teaching on it from the pulpit or in small groups. Unfortunately, the church tends to follow the individualistic bent covered in a prior chapter. This "what can I get out of it," consumer mentality of the culture dominates the choices we make; and has invaded many local churches. This attitude causes many to miss the sheer inner joy Christians feel and express when they learn the message of redemption and reconciliation that is spoken at the table. By failing to teach the great theme of redemption expressed at table worship we deny our new Christians the power of the table message that will provide them with healing and continual nourishment on the gospel and the presence of Jesus, the Bread of Life, who abides in them and them in Him. It is imperative that the enactment and gospel of the communion teaching be recovered.

Church history reflects that the Lord's Supper was the centerpiece of early Christian worship. Gathered around the table, fellow believers met with the Lord and each other in *unity*. Christ had expressed this type of humility and unity when He instituted the Supper (see Matthew 26:26-30; Mark 14:22-26; Luke 22:14-23). In 1 Corinthians 11, Paul gives explicit instructions concerning the Lord's Supper after being informed of violation of the spirit and purpose of the meal. He speaks of the revelation from Christ, which he delivered to the people:

*The teaching I gave you is the same teaching I received from the Lord: On the night when the Lord Jesus was handed over to be killed, He took bread and gave thanks for it. Then He broke the bread and said, "**This is my body; it is for you. Do this to remember me.**" In the same way, after they ate, Jesus took the cup. He said, "**This cup is the new agreement that is sealed with the blood of my death. When you drink this, do it to remember me.**" Every time you eat this bread and drink this cup you are telling others about the Lord's death until He comes. So a person who eats the bread or drinks the cup of the Lord in a way that is not worthy of it will be guilty of sinning against the body and the blood of the Lord. Look into your own hearts before you eat the bread and drink the cup, because all who eat the bread and drink the cup without recognizing the body eat and drink judgment against themselves. That is why many in your group are sick and weak and many have died. But if we judged ourselves in the right way, God would not judge us. But when the Lord judges us, he* *punishes us so that we will not be destroyed along with the world (vv. 17-32 NCV).*

- I received speaks of Paul's revelation from Christ.
- The Lord's Supper looks back to Christ's death and forward to His Second Coming (see Matthew 26:29; Mark 14:25; Luke 22:18).
- In an unworthy manner refers to the way in which a person eats the Lord's Supper.
- Sleep here refers to the death of Christians (see 15:18; 1 Thessalonians 4:15, 16).
- In the passage, Paul is referring to untimely death, a punishment suffered by some Christians who failed to examine themselves at the Lord's Supper (v. 28).
- If we would judge ourselves, God would not need to correct us. But when Christians are unwilling to do this self-examination, God Himself will chasten them. Some Christians avoid partaking of the Lord's Supper probably thinking; that to do so preempts God's chastening? "Do this in remembrance of Me."

The Bread of Life

The Jews therefore quarreled among themselves, saying, "How can this Man give us His flesh to eat?" Then Jesus said to them, *"Most assuredly, I say to you, unless you eat the flesh of the Son of man and drink His blood, you have no life in you. Whoever eats My flesh and drinks My blood has eternal life, and I will raise him up in the last day. For My flesh is food indeed, and My blood is drink indeed. He who eats My flesh and drinks My blood abides in Me, and I in him"* (John 6:52-57).

Few words in all the Scripture have been so misinterpreted by teachers, preachers, and religious theologians as this passage. The Jews were not the only people to strive about the meaning of these verses. God never intended these words to mean what man has declared. When people interpret the Scriptures to mean what they want it to mean, they are not only setting up their death, but are partaking of their poison, the doctrines of men.

Again, the "flesh and blood of the Son of man" simply means the sacrifices of His body, the shedding of His blood on the cross when He died for the sins of the whole world. The atonement Jesus made through His death; the satisfaction He gave through His suffering as our perfect, sinless substitute; the redemption He purchased through His blood by willingly enduring the penalty for our sins is the true meaning of the flesh and the blood of the Son of man. Can't you just picture the scorn and sarcasm among the Jews when Jesus made His claim to be the Bread of Life, then when He spoke of eating His flesh and drinking His blood naturally being in the flesh became furious. "Who does this fellow think He is? How can He give us His flesh to eat [cannibalize] and His blood to drink?" Like millions today, the Jews were determined to keep their spirituality in the natural realm. They refused to think in the realm of the supernatural; as a result many no longer walked with Jesus.

Eating and drinking here is with the heart, the spirit, soul, and body *by faith,* not by sight. The flesh and blood of Jesus means the vicarious sacrifice of His body on the cross. There is absolutely no salvation without this cardinal truth. Gaining an understanding in the Word of God on how the true Christian lives, we will have the meaning of eating His flesh and drinking His blood: In Romans 1:16, 17 KJV we read, *"For I am not ashamed of the gospel of Christ; for it is the power of God unto salvation to everyone that believeth; to the Jew first, and also to the Greek. For therein is the righteousness of God revealed from faith to faith; as it is written,* **the just shall live by faith."**

The justified individual—who possesses eternal life, lives that life by faith. How does he or she obtain that faith? "So then faith comes by hearing, and hearing by the Word of God" (Romans 10:17). Therefore, to eat the flesh and drink the blood of the Son of God is to appropriate His Word. Receiving the Word brings saving faith, and when we are saved by faith we "desire the sincere milk of the Word that we may grow thereby" (see 1 Peter 2:2).

We grow by feeding on the milk, meat, and bread of the Word. Thus, to eat the flesh and drink the blood of the Son of God is to receive and appropriate His Word into our very heart and life [godly spirituality] the engrafted Word that saves the soul, the incorruptible seed that brings eternal life! Notice the close, intimate relationship between Christ and the Christian—"*He . . . dwelleth in me, and I in Him*" *(see John 6:56 KJV)*. This intimate union between Christ and the Christian is borne out in the following Scripture:

> *There is therefore now no condemnation to them*
> *which are in Christ Jesus, who walk not after*
> *the flesh, but after the spirit (Romans 8:1).*

> *"To whom God would make known what is the riches*
> *of glory of this mystery among the gentiles: which is*
> **Christ in you,** *the hope of glory" (Colossians 1:27).*

> *"You are dead, and your life is hid with*
> *Christ in God" (Colossians 3:3).*

We know that food and drink keep the physical body alive and cause it to grow, and our food and drink become part of the body. The same is true in the spiritual sense. When we receive the Word of God, the living Word, we are appropriating Christ and He becomes part of us, the new creation (II Corinthians 5:17).

REFLECTION

My son, do not despise the chastening of the LORD
nor detest His correction;
for whom the LORD loves He corrects
just as a father the son in whom he delights
(Proverbs 3:11-12)

Review Responses (Chapter 10)

1. The most important thing I learned from this chapter is:

2. The area that I need to work on the most is:

3. I can apply this lesson to my life by:

4. Closing statement of Commitment:

CHAPTER 11

ANSWERED PRAYER

If I had known of any sin in my heart,
The Lord would not have listened to me
Psalm 66:18.

There can be absolutely no true godly spirituality without *answered prayer*. Above all prayer is a central means of edification. We carry out our edification mandate as we become a praying people, practicing the ministry and privilege of intercession (see James 5:16). We intercede for each other because as a kingdom of priests purchased by Christ (Revelation 5:10), each of us functions in the church as a priest.

In the Upper room Jesus provided a model for our intercession. *"My prayer is not that you take them out of the world,"* He said, *"But that you protect them from the evil one. They are not of the world, even as I am not of it. Sanctify them by the truth; your Word is truth"* (John 17:17).

Prayer lays hold of and releases God's willingness and power to act in accordance with the divine will on behalf of the creation, which He loves! Our petition becomes the cry for God to act in the present needy situation.

The Holy Place within the Tabernacle of Moses teaches in picture what we need to know about coming into the presence of

God in prayer and intercession and getting our prayers answered. In the holy place there was *"an altar to burn incense upon"* (see Exodus 30:1). A specific recipe was given by God for making the incense, which was to be used only in the tabernacle in the Lord's service.

The Picture

The psalmist said, *"Lord, I cry unto thee: make haste unto me; give ear unto my voice, when I cry unto thee. Let my prayer be set forth before thee as incense; and the lifting up of my hands as the evening sacrifice" (Psalm 141:1-2) KJV.* By connecting incense and prayer the psalmist shows how the ascending incense was the way he wanted his prayer to go up before God. He desired that his prayer be a fragrant and pleasant to God as incense, thus the picture of prayer in the Old Testament.

The New Testament also uses incense to picture prayer. In Revelation 5:8, *"The four beasts and the four and twenty elders fell down before the Lamb, having every one of them harps, and golden vials [censers] full of odors [incense], which are the prayers of the saints."[Brackets are mine].* This verse tells us the incense is the prayers of the saints, and not just a picture of prayer. Revelation 8:3-4 adds,

"And another angel came and stood at the altar,
having a golden censer;
and there was given unto him much incense,
that he should offer it with the prayers of all saints
upon the golden altar which was before the throne.
And the smoke of the incense,
which came with the prayers of the saints,
ascended up before God out of the angel's hand."

The smoke of the incense was offered with the saints' prayers, and the two came together before God. The two are aligned and given as the same thing in Revelation 5:8. The altar of incense then teaches us how to get our prayers answered. There are more instructions about prayer in the altar of incense than can be found in any other place in the Bible. Notice, this altar was placed just before the veil; which separated the holy place and Most Holy Place where God dwelt with His people (see Exodus 30:6). To offer incense the priest had to be in this place of worship before the altar. Two prerequisites for anyone coming into the holy place and to the altar of incense:

1) He had to go the brazen altar, the place of sacrifice, which pictures Calvary and of Christ's suffering, dying, and shedding His blood for our sins. Today *this means that anyone who wants to pray* must first be sure that he or she has been to Calvary, where by faith he or she has offered Christ as their Savior, Substitute and sacrifice for sins. The individual must claim Christ's blood to cleanse him or her from all sin before they can come into God's presence. As ministers of the Gospel we must be careful to insure that this teaching is understood thoroughly; especially by our new converts. An unsaved person has no access, no right, to come into God's presence in prayer and expect anything. The first prerequisite then is that a person must be *born again*. He or she must receive the sinless sacrifice, the Lamb of God for themselves as their personal Savior by faith. Remember you must have a sacrifice before you can come into God's presence; then your prayers can be heard and answered. Hebrews 10:19-20 says,

> *"Having therefore, brethren,*
> *boldness to enter into the holiest*
> *by the blood of Jesus by a new and living way,*
> *which He hath consecrated for us,*
> *through the veil,*
> *that is to say, His flesh."*

God invites us to "come boldly unto the throne of grace, that we may obtain mercy and find grace to help in time of need" (see Hebrews 4:16). But we do not come without the blood, without having claimed Jesus Christ's blood to cleanse us; allowing us to stand in the presence of a Holy God.

2) God said in Exodus 30:18-20, *"thou shalt also make a laver of brass, and his foot also of brass, to wash withal: and thou shalt put it between the tabernacle of the congregation and the altar, and thou shalt put water therein. For Aaron and his sons shall wash their hands and their feet thereat: when they go into the tabernacle of the congregation, they shall wash with water that they die not"* KJV.

The priests had to wash their hands and feet before entering the holy place to worship, to offer incense to the Lord. This was necessary that God said they had to do it **"lest they die."** The laver [Word of God] is the place of confession of sin for the Christian before he or she come into God's presence to worship or serve Him! The Christian must be *cleansed* from the daily defilement of sin. "If I regard iniquity in my heart, the Lord will not hear me" (see Psalm 66:18). Unconfessed sin in our lives is another reason, our prayers go unanswered. God says that we are sinners in need of forgiveness. To confess is to agree with Him, to admit that we are sinners in need of His mercy. If a Christian confesses his or her specific sins to God, He will forgive them and cleanse us from all unrighteousness (see 1 John 1:9). *But if we walk in the light as He is in the light, we have fellowship with one another, and the blood of Jesus Christ His Son cleanses us from all sin (1 John 1:7).*

Ungodly spirituality

Some Christians today are carrying grudges, envy, strife, jealousy, and animosity in their hearts; suffering loss of victory in their lives and seeing their prayers go unanswered. *The eyes of the Lord are upon the righteous, and His ears are open unto their cry. The face of the Lord is against them that do evil" (Psalm 34:15-16).* God says we should pray (see Luke 18:1) and that He is a God who hears prayer (see Psalm 65:2), but the prayer *must come* from those who have been washed—who are saved—and who have confessed their sins before they come into His presence. Listen, not just the unsaved have "the face of the Lord against them," but so do His own children who are walking in disobedience with unconfessed sin. To have our prayers answered we must confess and forsake every sin. There is an ungodly secularized spirituality of this world running rampart in many of the local churches causing fear and unbelief and when it is tolerated it eventually causes irreverence and disunity rather than the unity that the Lord desires.

Some Christians have prayed for divine healing in their bodies, others have asked for deliverance of loved ones, while still others have asked for jobs, better health, and finances, but many of these prayers have been in vain simply because there is still unconfessed sin in their lives. Christians must come to the truth in this matter of sins and realize there is no such thing as "pet sins" or "partial forgiveness." Like Cain people want to do it their way, without blood. The Scripture says, *"If we confess our sins, He is faithful and just to forgive us our sins and to cleanse us from all unrighteousness" (1 John 1:9).* "All unrighteousness" includes every sin. Again, confession means you agree with God concerning the sin and repent.

God's way and God's will

God is a holy God, and like the priest stood in the holy place to come to Him, for there he was in the place of fellowship with God. *God's way,* this is the place where prayer ascends to God and gets through to Him. To get our prayers answered we must spend time in fellowship with Him. *"If you abide in Me, and My words abide in you, you will ask what you desire, and it shall be done for you. By this My Father is glorified, that you bear much fruit; so you will be My disciples. As the father loved Me, I also have loved you; abide in My love. If you keep My commandments, you will abide in My love, just as I have kept My Father's commandments and abide in His love" (John 15:7-10).* This takes time. It means getting alone with God in prayer, fellowshipping with Him, delighting ourselves in the Lord. Set your affection on things above, not on things on the earth (see Colossians 3:2). *I am the vine, you are the branches, He who abides in Me, and I in him, bears much fruit; for without Me you can do nothing" (John 15:5).* Apart from Christ, a Christian cannot accomplish anything pertaining to true godly spiritually.

Being in the holy place also depicted being in *God's will*. It was God's will for the priests to go into the holy place and offer up incense. To get our prayers answered we too, must be in God's will, and we must pray in His will. "This is the confidence that we have in Him, that if we ask anything according to His will, He hears us." "And if we know that He hears us, whatever we ask, we know that we have the petitions that we have asked of Him" (1 John 5:14-15). It is imperative that all Christians learn, to pray in God's way and according to His will—you will not see your prayer go unanswered; that's a promise of God! If we are to get our prayers answered, it must be according to God's will, in the holy place, in fellowship with God, with no unconfessed sin in our lives.

Christ our Advocate

Christ is our Advocate; our prayer *must* go through Him to the Father. He is our Intercessor who, *"ever liveth to make intercession for us" (see Hebrews 7:25 KJV).* He is at the Father's right hand. There is power in prayer directed to God through Christ. If we have the "faith as a grain of mustard seed" (see Matthew 17:20), we can say to a mountain, "Be thou removed" (Mark 11:23 KJV) and it will. James says, "Is any among you afflicted? Let him pray"

(James 5:13). He tells us further that, "the prayer of faith shall save the sick, and the Lord shall raise him up" (v. 15).

There is power in prayer over physical sickness, so that God can intervene and work on our behalf. It's so sad today that few people truly tap into this power and see God work miracles in answer to prayer; and raise up the sick and afflicted. James summarizes it, *"The effectual fervent prayer of a righteous man availeth much" (see 5:16) KJV.* This availing is limited only by how much we pray. With these precious promises in prayer, it's no wonder James said, *"You have not because you ask not"* overlooking advantages of these blessings.

Too often prayer is a last resort, when it should be the first. We say, "I can't do anything else to help you, but I will pray for you," as though this meant the last result; reluctantly there's nothing else available. We live in an age of technological wonder even in the church, but as was the case with the chief priests and teachers of the law when King Herod queried them about the location of Jesus' birth. They were aware of Micah 5:2 and other prophecies about the Messiah; however their misconceptions kept them from taking the trip to see for themselves.

I pray that we will wake up because the world is on the brink of another such surprise as it deceptively plunges toward the "rapture" and the "Day of the Lord." King Herod had the male babies in Bethlehem killed trying to find the Truth, that was born right under his nose (see Matthew 2:16). I pray that God will help us to realize the power in prayer and use it to its fullest for His glory! Today God has made provision for the Christian in prayer in the Person of the Holy Spirit, who gives light, instruction and illumination in all spiritual things. *Likewise the Spirit also helps in our weaknesses. We do not know what we should pray for as we ought, but the Spirit Himself makes intercession for us with groanings which cannot be uttered. And we know that all things work together for good to those who love God, to those who are the called according to His purpose (see Romans 8:26, 28).*

Standing on the promises (Truth)

The people of this nation are scrambling today trying to find out what is? After following what is not for the past century; people are searching for "what is the truth." I believe this presents a great opportunity for Christians both individually and corporately, to really allow the Lord to be glorified through our testimonies and truly righteous witness. A closer look at our congregations reveals a large percentage of our people seems to have let Satan inoculate them against the truth of God's Word leaving them with blurred perceptions, doubt, fear, and for some of them little or no hope! How do we counter such ungodly spirituality? Do we continue to welcome unscriptural programs and new initiatives from the internet, local bookstores or denominational headquarters? Do we try a scattergun approach in the Sunday sermon hoping to hit as many people as we possibly can? Do we continue in the one thing we all do so well? Do nothing!

Jesus put great emphasis on, *"While it is day" (John 9:4);* which for Him signifies His messianic ministry, and the night refers to His crucifixion. I'm sure that you are visualizing Him at this moment "standing" steadfast on the Father's promises. This verse arose out of an incident wherein Jesus' critics challenged His miracle ministry and His spiritual purity after He healed a man born blind (see John 9:1-4). The perverse reasoning of the Pharisees placed them in a dilemma from which their only escape was to disprove the miracles that Jesus had performed (see vv. 8-12).

The resistance of the Pharisees was not unlike that which often is raised today against the present reality. Satan's deception has this secular (no Jesus Christ) society continuing to think that all problems and situations can be solved through science and rationalism, the secular worldview. It is shocking how rapidly secularism has advanced in Christendom, (Webster defines Christendom as the place where the church is located). It is not the church. Praise God! A *foundational* answer to such false reality is found in Jesus' response to His critics: *"Before Abraham was "I AM."* Christ's answer points to all of His Person and ministry, and to His own *unchanging* timelessness. This is a timeless message for us today. Jesus is not the great "I was" of centuries past, but He is the great "I AM," "the same yesterday, today, and forever" (see Hebrews 13:8). Every Christian should study the prophecies of the Bible. If you begin to prayerfully study today it would shock you to see how the course of this world is running according to the prophetic Books of Revelation, Daniel, Ezekiel and other books of the Bible. Most of all you will know that there is a God in heaven and He is very much in charge of the universe! Don't try to rationalize God. He has spoken in these last days through His Son, Jesus Christ. Hear Him!

In John 8:32 Jesus responds to the futile claim of the people that they are descendents of Abraham, because their deeds evidenced a lack of any moral relationship to Him. If they were *truly* children of God, they would reverence the Son of God. Instead their reaction to Him only revealed who they really were, Satan's children. What makes one acceptable to God? Believing in and loving His Son, Jesus Christ. The answer that I just penned will distinguish godly spirituality from ungodly spirituality every time!

Jesus [promised], *"If you abide in My word, you are My disciples indeed. And you shall [know] the truth, and the truth shall make you free" (John 8:31-32)*. The brackets are mine. Emphasis is placed on **know**. The Greek word is *ginosko (ghin-oce-koe)*; Strong's #1097: Ginosko is the knowledge that has an interception, a progress, and an attainment. It is the recognition of truth by personal experience. Jesus is saying you are free to the extent of the truth you know by personal experience with Jesus Christ.

The Only True God

In the Cross, Jesus reveals the Father to the world, that is, His love and justice, and that through Jesus' death on the cross, God would provide forgiveness of sins and give eternal life to all those who believe in His Son. This knowledge opposes all false gods.

And this is eternal life, that they may know You, the
only true God, and Jesus Christ whom You have sent
(John 17:3).

Jesus said, *"I am the way, [the truth], and the life. No one*
comes to the Father except through Me" (John 14:6). He is the
only way to the Father. He is the truth about God and the very life
of God. As such, He reveals *truth* to us and gives us life. Do you
truly know Him? Recognize that *knowing* Jesus is the only way to
God. By *knowing* Jesus, you know God.

REFLECTION

Deliver those who are drawn toward death,
and hold back those stumbling to the slaughter.
If you say,
"Surely we did not know this, does not He who
weighs the hearts consider it?" (Proverbs 24: 11-12).

Review Responses (Chapter 11)

1. The most important thing I learned from this chapter was:

2. The area that I need to work on the most is:

3. I can apply this lesson to my life by:

4. Closing statement of Commitment:

SECTION IV

CHRIST'S RETURN

CHAPTER 12

MADE HERSELF READY

Let us be glad and rejoice and give Him glory,
for the marriage of the Lamb has come,
and His wife has made herself ready
(Revelation 19:7).

Jesus loved the Church with an everlasting love. He laid down His life for the Church, He purchased it with His own blood (see Acts 20:28; Ephesians 5:25-27). The Church on earth has weathered many storms since her birth on the Day of Pentecost, and has longed for her lover, the Bridegroom, to appear in the clouds and call her up to meet Him. We will be caught up to meet our Savior in the air!

The Lamb's Wife Makes Herself Ready

Note in verse 7, *"His wife has made herself ready."* There are two kinds of readiness, and the New Testament Church is the subject of both:

1. God, in the exercise of His sovereign grace, makes the Bride
    ready for heaven and the glories of the New Jerusalem. We
    read, *"Giving thanks to the Father, who has qualified us*
    to be partakers of the inheritance of the saints in the light
    (Colossians 1:12). The word "qualified" means to be able or
    authorized for a task. Christians *can never* be qualified on
    their own; instead God *must make* then sufficient through
    Jesus Christ. The tense of the verb points to an act in the past
    rather than a process.

    Ordinarily to qualify for an event or a position, we have
    to prove ourselves. However the *inheritance* (see v. 5) that
    believers receive is *not one that they have earned*—but is based
    on being *qualified* by God. The Father qualifies us for eternal
    life with Him—whereas the Son will reward us at the end of
    the race (see Revelation 22:12). Many people smirk or kind
    of joke when addressed as *"saints"*—Paul frequently used the
    word in referring to born again believers (Christians)—get use
    to it!

2. All believers must **make themselves ready** before they enter
    eternal glory, the home of the redeemed. Before the saints are
    ready to reign with Christ, certain situations must be put right.
    The Bible clearly states that some who stand before Jesus will
    be *ashamed* of themselves:

    "And now little children, abide in Him; that when He shall
    appear *(when He comes again)*, we may have confidence, and
    not be ashamed before Him at His coming" (1 John 2:28).
    Certainly this verse refers to believers. *There must be a period*
    of preparation at the judgment seat of Christ where the Bride
    will be given an opportunity to prepare herself (Today?) to be
    cleansed; and the believers will be rewarded according to the
    record of their works.

There are many carnal Christians who live worldly and indifferent lives, who will have to pass through the fires of that judgment seat before they are ready to return with the Lord to reign on the earth. All mistakes and misunderstandings will be rectified, the dross will be burned, and the saints will be rewarded for faithful stewardship. This will precede the marriage of the Lamb.

Thus, His wife has made herself ready, and will pass from the judgment seat of Christ into the loving presence of the Lamb—to become His Bride forever. As noted earlier, there are many saved people who will be ashamed at the coming of the Lord; for they did not obey His Great Commission.

Salvation is God's free gift. Rewards which are to be received at the judgment seat of Christ must be *earned* through faithful stewardship which includes personal and corporate evangelism. Paul counsels,

*"For other foundation can no man lay than that is laid, which is Jesus Christ. Now if any man build upon this foundation gold, silver, precious stones, wood, hay, stubbles; everyman's work shall be made manifest: for the day shall declare it, because it shall be revealed by fire; and the **fire shall try every man's work of what sort it is.** If any man's work abides which he hath built thereupon, he shall receive a reward. If any man's work shall be burned, he shall suffer loss: but he himself shall be saved; yet so as by fire (1 Corinthians 3:11-15 KJV).*

Yes, a believer can lose his or her reward; but praise God Jesus is our salvation! When by faith we place our hand in His precious nail-scarred hand, He is able to keep us through His mighty power. We are warned to hold fast that which we have, that we lose not our crown—but a crown is certainly not our salvation. There are five crowns mentioned in the New Testament which can be earned by a believer through faithful stewardship:

1. The incorruptible Crown—"temperance" (1 Corinthians 9:25)
2. The crown of rejoicing—"soul-winning" (1 Thessalonians 2:19)
3. The Crown of righteousness—"being faithful" (II Timothy 4:8)
4. The crown of life—"stand temptation" (James 1:12)
5. The crown of glory—"feeding the flock" (1 Peter 5:4)

If you do a thorough study of each of the Scriptures, you will find clearly stated the requirements for coming into possession of one (or all five) of these crowns. Some Christians will receive a full reward. Others will lose their reward, and their works will be burned up. I believe the most common danger among Christians today is unfaithfulness to the *pure Gospel*. Please carefully study the Second Epistle of John—just thirteen short verses, and hear what the Spirit is saying to you. No born again individual should be found in a church that is not true to the pure gospel of Christ nor support any preacher or ministry who denies the faith. What faith you might ask? "The faith" [refers to the Bible] once delivered to the saints, as recorded in the Book of Jude. *"Know ye not that they which run in a race run all, but one receiveth the prize? So run, that ye may obtain" (1 Corinthians 9:24 KJV)*. Be faithful!

Today true Christians and true preachers of the gospel are pushed around by the carnal elements in many local churches. One day that will be over. They will no longer be called fanatics and antiquated religious crackpots. Today thousands of Spirit-filled Christians are being run out of churches they helped to build. In spite of it all we still have joy! If we walk in the Spirit, fellowship with the Spirit, and listen to the Spirit, we will *not* become discouraged in these trying days.

What will you be doing when Jesus Comes?

I have heard this question asked in a song as well as seen it in various writings. Sometimes it is asked in jest. However, it is a very important question individually and corporately. In fact, rewards at the judgment seat of Christ will be determined by our faithfulness to Christ while we are waiting on His return.

Have the churches been faithful witnesses? (That includes your church). Has your church been a true witness to the treasures of His divine grace? Has your church been a true witness to the character of God? Is the living expression of Christ visible in the members of the local assembly? Is your church the light and salt of the community? Jesus has been completely shut out of many churches today—however, He seeks entrance for the purpose of renewed fellowship. He remains at the door knocking (see Revelation 3:20).

In Revelation 2-3, we find letters written to the seven churches two of which seem to be representative of the church today. The Lord had nothing but *commendation* for one, the church in Philadelphia and nothing but *condemnation* for the second one, the church of the Laodiceans.

To the church in Philadelphia:

Jesus assures the true believers in Philadelphia that he will make the pretenders, the counterfeit church members, those who profess but do not possess, to come and worship at the feet of the true church (see v. 9).

*"Because thou hast **kept the word** of my patience, I also will **keep thee from the hour of temptation**, which shall come upon all the world, to try them that dwell upon the earth. Behold, I come quickly: hold that fast which thou hast, that no man take your crown (vv. 10-11 KJV).*

Two things are pointed out in this passage:

- First—"Because thou hast kept the word of my patience . . . ." The Spirit is saying here, "Because you have been true to the pure Word of God." If the devil could discredit the Word of God, the foundation of Christianity would crumble and Satan could destroy the Church of the Living God. But that will never happen! The Word of God is the solid Rock!

- Second—This church had not only kept the Word, but they had also kept His name. They had not denied, but had lifted up the name of Jesus; that is lifted up in the Word—the name of Jesus that at the sound of which every knee shall bow in heaven, in earth, and things under the earth (Philippians 2:10).

"I also will keep thee from the hour of temptation."

There are many ideas and doctrines concerning the Church and the Great Tribulation that shall come upon the earth, during the reign of the Antichrist. Some teach that the church will go through the first half of the Tribulation then it will be raptured (mid-tribulation). Others teach that the church will go through the entire Tribulation then it will be raptured (post-tribulation). I teach along with many others teachers, *the truth;* that is the church will be raptured *prior (pre-tribulation)* to the appearing of the Antichrist, *before the beginning* of the Tribulation, *"the hour of temptation that shall come upon all the world to try them that dwell upon the earth."*

True Christians keep the Word and true Christians confess the name of Jesus. Thus, the promise to those in Philadelphia is, "Because thou hast kept the word of my patience, I will keep thee from the hour of temptation that will come upon all the earth. Another Scriptural proof: *"For God hath not appointed us to wrath, but to obtain salvation by our Lord Jesus Christ"*

(1 Thessalonians 5:9 KJV). In chapters one through three of Revelation the church is mentioned nineteen times. After chapter four the Tribulation is described, but the church is not mentioned. The Church is looking for Christ, our Lord and Savior not for the Antichrist!

Verses12 and 13 KJV: "Him that overcometh will I make a pillar in the temple of my God, and he shall go no more out: and I will write upon him the name of my God, and the name of the city of my God, which is new Jerusalem, which cometh down out of heaven from my God: and I will write upon him my new name. He that hath an ear let him hear what the Spirit saith to the churches."

The Philadelphia church is The Church (**without** spot) that will be *raptured out* of the earth. Notice, 1 Thessalonians 4:16-18 says, *"For the Lord himself shall descend from heaven with a shout, with the voice of the archangel, and with the trump of God: and the dead in Christ shall arise first: Then we which are alive and remain shall be caught up together with them in the clouds, to meet the Lord in the air: and so shall we ever be with the Lord. Wherefore comfort one another with these words."*

In the Bible, the Lord is often accompanied by clouds, signifying His glory (see Psalm 68:4; 97:2). The most important result is that *we will always be with the Lord!* This wonderful promise is to be a comfort to the Thessalonians and to all Christians. The sentence is in the present tense, indicating that it should be a constant comfort to us to think each day that the Lord may come. At the same time the Laodiceans will be *spewed out.*

Each of the seven churches is identical to a period of church history behind us, up to Philadelphia and the church of the Laodiceans. I believe we are now living in the very hour of the coming of the Son of God for The Church. Those who study prophecy will agree that every prophecy having to do with the coming of the Lord has been fulfilled, or is being fulfilled today right before our very eyes! One of these days the Rapture will take place and it will all be over, *"In the twinkling of an eye"* (see 1 Corinthians 15:51-52). Give Him praise!

To the Church of the Laodiceans

The final church mentioned in Revelation is the *lukewarm church of the Laodiceans,* unlike the other six churches mentioned by their City's location, this church is identified as the people's church (of the Laodiceans). This church will be in existence when Christ returns. Cold water is refreshing hot water is useful for medical purposes. Lukewarm water is good for nothing.

A great number of churches worldwide are lukewarm in these perilous days of the twenty-first century. This church assumed it had need of nothing because it had expensive garments and was well-clothed, when it was really spiritually naked. Note the similarities between the organized Christian community today and the Laodicean church:

- The church was outwardly impressive; so they thought that made them spiritual; therefore they assumed their half-hearted efforts were pleasing to Christ.
- It had all the trappings of wealth—but something was missing.
- The church had been lulled to sleep with all of this prestige.
- The members were rich in material goods, but spiritually poor.
- The Lord had nothing positive to say about this church; in fact it made Him sick.
- It's so interesting that God looks at apostasy and gets angry—but He looks at indifference and becomes sick.
- The preaching of that church was compromising.
- The pastor probably didn't want to upset the congregation.
- The pastor's main concerns were the number of members and the offering plate.
- The Lord says, ". . . . because you are lukewarm, neither hot nor cold—I will spit you out of my mouth" (Revelation 3:16). How does this description of the Laodicean's church compare with your church?

We are afraid of being on fire for the Lord; because we don't want to be labeled as fanatics and yet in every other area of life we throw off proper manners and exude enthusiasm. It is expected of everyone at the football game. But in our Christian experience most of us are like jello or an overcooked noodle.

I read about an eccentric man who walked around town with a sandwich sign slung over his shoulders. The front of the sign said: "I am a fool for Christ!" As he walked the streets, he was ridiculed by those who saw the front of his placard, until he had passed by and they read what was written on the back: "Whose fool are you?"

Christ gave us specific prescriptions for the sick church of the last days. He wrote them out clearly, so that anyone could read the directions:

- First He said, "Those whom I love I rebuke and discipline. So be earnest and repent" (Revelation 3:19). He did not say, "Think about it," or "When you get around to it." Do it now!
- Another prescription was given for their spiritual poverty. He told them to no longer trust in their bank accounts (earthly economy); but come to God for His riches (kingdom economy). Trust Him for everything!

- The next prescription was for the cure of spiritual blindness. Revelation 3:18 refers to "healing salve of repentance to put on your eyes, so you can see."

- The final prescription is a positive cure for compromise, poverty, nakedness, and blindness to spiritual realities.

As we work to maintain the health and spirituality of the church, we enable the body to become all God designed it to be: a glorious church, not having spot or wrinkle or any such thing, but that she should be holy and without blemish (see Ephesians 5:27). Jesus said, *"He who overcomes I will grant to sit with Me on My throne as I also overcame and sat down with My Father on His throne" (v. 21).*

REFLECTION

The fear of the LORD is the beginning of wisdom,
and the knowledge of the Holy One is understanding
(Proverbs 9:10).

Review Responses (Chapter 12)

1. The most important thing I learned from this chapter was:

2. The area that I need to work on the most is:

3. I can apply this lesson to my life by:

4. Closing statement of commitment:

CHAPTER 13

THE POWER OF THE RESURRECTION

*That I may know Him and the power of His
resurrection, and the fellowship of His sufferings, being
conformed to His death (see Philippians 3:10).*

Peter preached the gospel of Jesus Christ on the Day of Pentecost
and three thousand souls received the Word and were saved—a
few days later after hearing and receiving the gospel another
five thousand believers were added to the church. I have read
the estimates of some that say, Peter's sermon was preached in
about three minutes. Whether that is fact or not—how many
churches today are receiving three thousand (truly born again)
souls during their entire existence on earth? Why are people not
eager to join the church today? I think the answer to these and
many other questions that the churches face today can be traced
to *"having a form of godliness but denying its power" (see 2
Timothy 3:5).* "Form" refers to outward shape or appearance.
Like the unbelieving scribes and Pharisees, false teachers and their
followers are concerned with mere external appearances. The
outward *form* of ungodly spirituality and virtues make them all
the more dangerous (see Matthew 23:25; Titus 1:16).

Church Operational Forms

As we study the early church, it becomes obvious that they centered their apologetic and spirituality on the death and resurrection of Christ. After the resurrection of Jesus Christ everything changed as this was now a transition period. Many times when the church in (Acts 2:42-47) is mentioned someone will quickly pipe up, "but that was for the Jewish church; or mention *(signs and wonders or miracles)*, and you are told, "Those were here only for a season to validate the apostles' divinely ordained position." Lest we forget, the Scripture says, *"These signs **shall** follow them that believe" (Mark 16:17)*. I would venture to say that much of the failure in our churches today is the result of people misinterpreting biblical truths, and redefining the meaning and priority of our New Testament model. To ignore the New Testament model we really have a shaky foundation if any for the church. Notice their four essential foundational objectives for the church:

- *The apostles' doctrine*—the foundational content for the believers' godly spirituality and maturity was from the Scripture. God revealed truth to the apostles, which they received and taught faithfully; those who received the apostles' doctrine were *baptized* [this method of operation remains to this day] (study very carefully John 14:26; 15:26-27; 16:13).

- *Fellowship*—Because Christians became partners with Jesus Christ and all other believers (see 1 John 1:3; 1 Corinthians 1:9) it becomes our spiritual duty to love, share, and encourage one another to righteousness and obedience (Study Romans 12:10; 13:8; 15:5; Galatians 5:13; Ephesians 4:2, 25; 5:21; Colossians 3:9).

- *Breaking of bread*—A reference to the Lord's Supper or Communion which is *mandatory* for all Christians to observe. Jesus did not merely suggest that we participate.

He commanded that we do it (study 1 Corinthians 11:24-29; also review chapter 10 of this book).

- *Prayers*—of the individual believers and the church corporately and or small groups (study Acts 1:14, 24; 4:24-31; John 14:13-14; review chapter 11 of this book).

These four objectives are just as foundational and essential for a viable church today as they were in the first century. Additionally, I see significance in the order of their listing in verse 42! This passage ends in verse 47 with: *"And the Lord added to the church daily those who were being saved."* If the Lord is not adding to your church, perhaps one or more of the essentials above are being neglected or improperly taught and prioritized. The resurrection of Jesus Christ marked the beginning of a new era for the church. Our Lord Jesus Christ requires every member of His body to participate in these tasks effectively with resurrection power, as God intended it to be done. Listed below are some of the changes made immediately in the young church:

- The day of Worship was changed from the Jewish Sabbath to the first day of the week (resurrection Sunday!).
- The essence of worship became a celebration of His resurrection.
- There was a move from law to grace.
- Believers began to live in their baptism and resurrection, in Christ.
- The tithers under the law became cheerful givers under grace.
- Jesus told the church what they were "to be" and what they were "to do" in the Great Commandment and the Great commission (they became global and missionary).

The Great Commandment and the Great Commission

In Acts 1:1 we read, *". . . . all that Jesus began both to do and to teach."* Though the church began at Pentecost it was not *fully* revealed by God until later, primarily through the writings of the apostle Paul. Christ had promised to build His church (Matthew 16:18); and shortly there afterward, He gave the apostle Peter the "keys of the kingdom of heaven" (Matthew 16:19). Peter used these "keys" in opening the doors of faith to the *Jews* at Pentecost (see Acts 2), to the *Samaritans* (see Acts 8), and to the *Gentiles* (see Acts 10). The first seven chapters of the Book of Acts cover a transition period, with Israel moving off the scene as the church, and the Gospel of grace moved onto the scene (in time from Jerusalem to the uttermost parts of the earth).

Christ promised the apostles the baptism of the Holy Spirit (see Acts 1:5, 8), that took place at Pentecost (Acts 2, see 1 Corinthians 12:13) and in the home of Cornelius (Acts 10:45, see Acts 11:15-17). These *two* events included both *Jews* and *Gentiles* as a result the *body of Christ* was formed. In Romans 9-11 Paul explains, God had set aside Israel so that *"the fullness of the Gentiles* (see Romans 11:25) might be realized through the ministry of the church.

Many call the Book of Acts "The Acts of the Holy Spirit." Notice the work of the Holy Spirit in the church as the book progresses from Jewish ground to Church ground:

- Peter tells the Jews to repent, believe on Christ, be baptized and receive the Holy Spirit (see Acts 2:38).
- Peter prays for the Samaritans to receive the Spirit, lays hands on them, and they receive the gift of the Holy Spirit (see Acts 8:14-15).
- The Holy Spirit comes on the Gentiles when they accept Christ (see Acts 10:44).

- God's pattern for *today:* hear the Word, believe and receive the Gospel of Christ, receive the Holy Spirit and then be baptized as evidence of your faith.
- The Holy Spirit was the source and power of Jesus' earthly ministry (see Matthew 4:1; 12:18; Mark 1:12; Luke 3:22; 4:1, 14, 18).
- The Holy Spirit was the source and power of the apostles' ministries (see Luke 24:49; John 14:16, 17; 16:7)
- The Holy Spirit is the source and power in the New Testament church's ministry today (see John 14-16; Acts 1:8).

There are many churches today that operate without acknowledging the Holy Spirit's place and ministry in the Church. God forbid! The true church and godly spirituality realizes that without His presence and work we cannot be the church and therefore would only foster an ungodly spirituality. Christ said the Holy Spirit would lead and guide us (His church into all truth)! He is the Spirit of Truth! So the true church understands that living our spirituality through love and obedience to our Lord by keeping God's Great Commandment Matthew 22:37-40) and Great Commission (Matthew 28:19-20):

> *Love the Lord your God with all your heart and with all your soul and with all your mind . . . . Love your neighbor as yourself. All the Law and the Prophets hang on these two commandment (Matthew 22:37-40).*

Since we discussed this legal question earlier, we'll just sum up by saying that love for God and love for your neighbor sums up the entire Law (see Romans 13:8-10). We should never debate as the Pharisees did, but just obey and make sure we love God and others. This is truly the heart of godly spirituality. Of course, no one can love God apart from knowing Jesus Christ as Lord and Savior (see John 8:42). And when you know and love God, the love of God will be seen and shared with others (Romans 5:5).

Go and make disciples of all nations, baptizing them in the name of the Father and of the Son and of the Holy Spirit, and teaching them to obey everything I have commanded you (Matthew 28:19-20).

Later, among His last words to His disciples, Jesus gave the Great Commission to them and to the church containing three tasks:

- Go make disciples.
- Baptize them.
- Teach them *to obey* everything that He had taught.

Every church is defined by her commitment to these God assigned tasks for His church to accomplish; we say it this way in the Bread of Life Ministries Int'l:

- Love God.
- Love people.
- Win people to Christ and the community.
- Teach and train them for service.
- Send them into the service of the Lord.

A Change must come (When we believe!)

It grieves me greatly as I observe professionals trying to treat inner maladies in people through outward means; attempting to cure spiritual problems with rationalistic and scientific methods—giving little or no consideration to the healing ministries of the church. Numerous published medical opinions have surfaced concerning many patients whose conditions were actually spiritual (inner) and not physical. We all know that we have an inner life (consisting of our *spirit* and *soul*). This life consists of our passions, desires, temptations, thoughts, selfishness and other stuff that even we are not aware of. In the *natural man,* all of the above mentioned items loom in their *souls* (which consists of our mind, emotions, and will). Man's medicines help in our physical conditions, but only God can heal us. It's amazing the number of medical professionals who have made this claim and promote prayer for healing.

Many patients today admit that their condition is beyond man's ability and select one or more of the following three options:

- They continue a course of prescriptions and treatments without possible cure.
- They seek spiritual cures through various medians and religious journeys.
- They seek spiritual relief through a relationship with God in Christ.

Using option three to enter our faith through grace will bring the divine nature of God and the resurrection power of Christ to bear on all of life's circumstances; all through the Holy Spirit in regeneration (see John 3:3, 16).

Regeneration

Therefore, just as through one man sin entered the world, and death through sin, and thus death spread to all men, because all sinned (Romans 5:12). In this passage which runs through v. 21, Paul sets out to show how one man's death can provide salvation for many. When Adam sinned all humankind sinned being in his loins (see v. 18; Hebrews 7:7-10). His sin transformed his *inner nature* and brought spiritual death and depravity, that sinful nature and propensity to sin would be passed on to make all humanity sinners by nature. Therefore, humans are not sinners because they sin—but rather they sin because they are sinners.

In Titus 3:5-7, Paul tells us salvation is, *not by works of righteousness which we have done, but according to His mercy He saved us, through the washing of regeneration and renewing of the Holy Spirit, whom He poured out on us abundantly through Jesus Christ our Savior, that having been justified by His grace we should become heirs according to the hope of eternal life.* Regeneration brings divine cleansing from sin and the gift of new Spirit-generated life through our born again spirit (see John 3:3).

"If when we were enemies we were reconciled to God through the death of His Son, much more, having been reconciled, we shall be saved by His life" (Romans 5:10). When we were God's enemies, Christ was able by His death to reconcile us to God. Certainly now that we are God's children, the Savior can keep us by His living resurrection power!

The Next Step

I meet more and more Christians who do not belong to any local church. Many of their reasons are not valid or let me say it this way; they are not spiritual. I hear them say things like:

- Someone hurt my feelings.
- Services are too long.
- I'm sick of tradition.
- I'm not being spiritually fed.
- They won't let me do anything.
- There are too many clichés.
- They are partial to certain people.
- My career keeps me from getting involved.

I think these are merely sensual excuses with little validity. When you trusted Christ as your Savior, something happened within you. According to 2 Corinthians 5:17; you became a completely new creation *within*. You gained a new nature (see 2 Peter 1:4), new motivation, and new interests. Your soul (mind, will, and emotions) should no longer be blinded to the truth of God's Word nor held in bondage to fleshly lust; because the love of God has been poured out in our hearts by the Holy Spirit who was given to us (Romans 5:5; 8:9). God demonstrates His love toward us in that while we were still sinners, Christ died for us (v. 8). Remember, God loves us just the way we are, but He loves us too much to leave us the way we are (see John 15:16; Philippians 1:6)

The Holy Spirit encourages the believer in their hope in God. Therefore, your interests begin to shift from yourself to others; and from the things of the flesh to the things of God. Remembering the four essentials discussed earlier, you will join a new group of people for fellowship. You can actually be more open to confess your faults. And this new family relationship will open to you an entirely new realm you never realized before. Remember the church at Philadelphia is the church without spot (the rapture church). Seek a personal manifestation of Christ; by moving from knowledge about Him to a personal acquaintance with Him.

REFLECTION

All the ways of a man are pure in his own eyes,
but the LORD weighs the spirits
(Proverbs 16:2).

Review Responses (Chapter 13)

1. The most important thing I learned from this chapter was:

2. The area that I need to work on the most is:

3. I can apply this lesson to my life by:

4. Closing statement of Commitment:

CHAPTER 14

IN THE LORD'S SERVICE

And He Himself gave some to be apostles, some prophets, some evangelists, and some pastors, and teachers for the equipping of the saints for the work of ministry, for the edifying of the body of Christ, till we all come to the unity of the faith and the knowledge of the Son of God, to a perfect man, to the measure of the stature of the fullness of Christ, that we should no longer be children, tossed to and fro and carried about with every wind of doctrine, by the trickery of men, in the cunning craftiness of deceitful plotting (Ephesians 4:11-14).

The belief that apostles and prophets were phased out when the writing of the New Testament was completed has really opened the door for the shenanigans and confusion caused by Satan's children mentioned in the Scripture above. Many people are left not knowing what to believe. Equipping refers to *restoring* something to its *original* condition, meaning the materials used in the process must be the same as the original. In this context, it refers to leading Christians from conversion to maturity. Scripture is the *key* to this process. In 2 Timothy 3:16-17, Paul reminds, *All Scripture is given by inspiration of God, and is profitable for doctrine, for reproof, for correction, for instruction in righteousness, that the man* [or woman] *may be complete, thoroughly **equipped** for every good work.* Brackets mine.

The Abiding Life

God cleanses us through the **Word**, chastening us to make us more fruitful, which helps to explain why dedicated Christians go through trials. The Christian's godly spirituality moves from producing "fruit" to "more fruit" to "much fruit" to the glory of God (see John 15:3). The evidences of the "abiding life," true spirituality are:

- a sense of the Savior's love
- obedience to the Word
- answered prayer
- and joy

Through the extended metaphor of the vine and branches, Jesus set forth the basis of the Christian's true spirituality. Jesus used the imagery of agricultural life at the time, vine crops. He specifically identified Himself as the *"true vine"* and the *"vinedresser"* or caretaker of the vine. The vine has two types of branches:

- Those that bear fruit are the [genuine believers down through the ages] (see vv. 2, 8).
- Those that do not bear fruit are those who [profess but do not possess] they have no life in the vine (see vv. 2, 6).
- The image of non-fruit-bearing branches being burned pictures eschatological judgment and eternal rejection (see Ezekiel 15:6-8).

True believers obey the Lord's commands, submitting to His Word (see John 14:21, 23). Because of their commitment to God's Word, they are devoted to His will, thus their prayers are fruitful (see John 14:13, 14), which puts the glory of God on display for all to see as He answers. Just as Jesus maintained that His obedience to the Father was the basis of His joy, so also the Christians who are obedient to His commandments will experience the same joy (see John 17:13).

The Pattern for the Church

We can see from what I have written so far, the Book of Acts written by Holy Spirit inspired writers did record the necessary teachings, experiences, and ministry for the New Testament church. The church is not a man-made entity, nor does it operate on natural laws or religious forms. The blueprint and pattern recorded in Acts portrays the Church as a *supernatural people* operating in supernatural principles. As the foundational church, everything found in the Book of Acts including the truths, principles, gifts, fruit of the Spirit, the miracles and ministries of the apostles, prophets, evangelist, pastor, and teacher were intended for the whole Church Age. That is why it is so important that we yield ourselves to the Holy Spirit and let Him change our traditional mind-sets and the status quo. One of the tenants of Jesus' Great Commission to the church states, *But you shall receive power when the Holy Spirit has come upon you; and you shall be witnesses to Me in Jerusalem, and in Judea and Samaria, and to the end of the earth (Acts 1:8).*

The Power of the Church

The Lord ascended having fulfilled all prophecies and all of His divinely ordained work of redemption. He gained the authority and sovereignty to rule the Church, and assign gifts (see Ephesians 4:7-8) to those He has called into service in His church. He gave not only gifts to people, but He also gave people who were gifts (see v. 11):

- apostles
- prophets
- evangelists
- pastors
- teachers

He gave them to equip the saints for the work of ministry:

- The edifying of the body of Christ.
- Bringing the saints into the knowledge of the Son of God.
- Bringing the saints to maturity in Christ.
- Ensuring that the saints learn discernment (see 1 Thessalonians 5:21, 22); so they are no longer carried about by deceitful false teachers in the church.
- Teaching the saints sound doctrine so they no longer fall for the trickery and craftiness of men and women.

Christians are to be completely yielded and obedient to the will of the Lord. The kingdom of God has arrived on earth and is in the believer. Romans 14:17 says, *"The kingdom of God is not eating and drinking, but righteousness and peace and joy in the Holy Spirit."* The kingdom of heaven then, does not consist of external things like food and drink, but in spiritual realities: First of all, *"the kingdom of God is not meat and drink;"* but the kingdom of God is first, *"righteousness,"* then *"peace,"* and third, *"joy in the Holy Ghost."*

- There can be no peace without righteousness.
- There can be no joy without peace and righteousness.

When we have been justified by faith we enter into peace with God and this peace with God leads to joy through our Lord Jesus Christ, and rejoices in hope to the glory of God. We glorify God when we do His will! Christians are subject to His control through the power of the Holy Spirit. Therefore, they are to be Christlike in all areas of their spirituality (life) growing up into Him (see

Galatians 2:20; Philippians 1:21). Christians are most effective when they proclaim the truth in love. It has been said, love makes truth palatable, while truth makes love practical. Truth without love can destroy a person by its brutality, while love without truth can destroy a person by its insincerity. Truth without love is powerless to change lives, while love without truth can change them in the wrong direction. Without spiritual maturity, the truth can be cold and love little more than sentimentality.

Restoring Koinonia

Great damage is being done to the church and the cause of Christ by Christians with an unhealthy, ungodly spirituality who attempt to carry out evangelistic or helping ministry with great zeal but without true godly love in their own hearts. Burdened with unresolved issues and problems in their own lives; these Christians often display unhealthy and unrecognized hypocrisy, prejudices, and works of the flesh bringing the body of Christ and the Gospel of Christ to shame in the world.

Paul uses an intentional exaggeration to illustrate the *uselessness* of each of the gifts listed above without love (see 1 Corinthians 13:1). What is terribly missing in so many churches is the *experience* of what the old church called "Christian love" [*agape*] and "fellowship" [*koinonia*] in the Greek. It is that warm "one another" love and fellowship which is defined in the New Testament. The New Testament puts great emphasis on the need for Christians to know *"one another"* closely and intimately enough to be able to bear one another's burdens, confess faults to one another, encourage, exhort, and admonish one another; and to minister to one another with Word, song, and prayer [true unity]. There are over fifty *"one another statements"* and *"commands"* in the New Testament which call us to a special kind of life together—what we call in this book "godly spirituality." These statements and commands are in the (NIV):

- "Be at peace with each other" (Mark 9:50).
- "Wash one another's feet" (John 13:14).
- "Love one another" (John 18:34).
- "Love one another" (John 13:35).
- "Love each other" (John 15:12).
- "Love each other" (John 15:17).
- "Be devoted to one another in brotherly love" (Romans 12:10).
- "Honor one another above yourselves" (Romans 12:10).
- "Live in harmony with one another" (Romans 12:16).
- "Love one another" (Romans 13:8).
- "Stop passing judgment on one another" (Romans 14:13).
- "Accept one another, then, just as Christ accepted you" (Romans 15:7).
- "Instruct one another" (Romans 15:14).
- "Greet one another with a holy kiss" (Romans 16:16).
- "When you come together to eat, wait for one other" (1 Corinthians 11:33).
- "Have equal concern for one another" (1 Corinthians 12:25).
- "Greet one another with a holy kiss" (1 Corinthians 16:20).
- "Greet one another with a holy kiss" (2 Corinthians 13:12).
- "Serve one another in love" (Galatians 5:18).
- "If you keep on biting and devouring one another . . . . You will be destroyed by each other" (Galatians 5:15).
- "Let us not become conceited, provoking and envying one another" Galatians 5:26).
- "Carry one another's burden" (Galatians 6:2).
- "Be patient with one another in love" (Ephesians 4:2).
- "Be kind and compassionate to one another" (Ephesians 4:32).
- "Forgiving one another" (Ephesians 4:32).
- "Speak to one another with psalms, hymns, and spiritual songs" (Ephesians 5:19).
- "Submit to one another out of reverence for Christ" (Ephesians 5:21).

- "In humility consider others better than yourselves" (Philippians 2:3).
- "Do not lie to one another" (Colossians 3:9).
- "Bear with one another" (Colossians 3:13).
- "Forgive whatever grievances you may have against one another" (Colossians 3:13).
- "Teach one another" (Colossians 3:16).
- "Admonish one another" (Colossians 3:16).
- "Make your love increase and overflow for one other" (1 Thessalonians 3:12).
- "Love one other" (1 Thessalonians 4:9).
- "Encourage one other" (1 Thessalonians 4:18).
- "Encourage one another" (1 Thessalonians 5:11).
- "Build one other up" (1 Thessalonians 5:11).
- "Encourage one another daily" (Hebrews 3:13).
- "Spur one another on toward love and good deeds" (Hebrews 10:24).
- "Encourage one another" (Hebrews 10:25).
- ""Do not slander one another" (James 4:11).
- "Don't grumble against one other" (James 5:9).
- "Confess your sins to one other" (James 5:16).
- "Pray for one another" (James 5:16).
- "Love one another deeply from the heart" (1 Peter 1:22).
- "Live in harmony with one another" (1 Peter 3:8).
- "Love one other deeply" (1 Peter 4:8).
- "Offer hospitality to one another without grumbling" (1 Peter 4:9).
- "Each one should use whatever gift he has received to serve one another" (1 Peter 4:10).
- "Clothe yourselves with humility toward one another" (1 Peter 5:5).
- "Greet one another with a kiss of love" (1 Peter 5:14).
- "Love one another" (1 John 3:11).
- "Love one another" (1 John 3:23).
- "Love one another" (1 John 4:7).
- "Love one another" (1 John 4:11).

- "Love one another" (1 John 4:12).
- "Love one another" (2 John 5).

It is apparent, these "one another" ministries in the body of Christ are very important to God, since He speaks of them so frequently in His Word. Certainly church leaders should make room for and encourage this type of ministry. This kind of interchange is difficult but not impossible with a structural change of the traditional church programs and methods of operation; as led by the Spirit of course. This was precisely in line with the exhortation of Jesus to His disciples: *"A new commandment I give to you, that you love one another; even as I have loved you, that you also love one another. By this all men will know that you are My disciples, if you have love for one another"* (John 13:34-35).

The early church was established upon a twofold witness as the means of reaching and impressing an unbelieving world: Speaking the truth (Gospel) in love, *kerygma* (proclamation) and *koinonia* (fellowship). It was the *combination* of the two that made the church so powerful and effective. *"In the mouth of two or three witnesses shall every word be established"* (Matthew 18:16 KJV). This combination prompted the much-quoted remark of a pagan writer: "How these Christians love one another!"

Many of today's churches have managed to do away with true New Testament koinoinia almost completely, reducing the witness of the church to proclamation *(kerygma)* alone. In doing so, the church has removed the major safeguard [true unity] to the health of the church's spirituality from within, and greatly weakened its effectiveness before the world without. In many eyes this has made the church irrelevant and useless in the world. God forbid! Koinoinia calls for love, honesty, and openness with other Christians. This kind of honesty would greatly assist in healing to individuals and family members also.

When this kind of love, sharing and burden bearing takes place in the church, the leadership will be relieved of much of the counseling and crisis intervention that normally confront them. Many spiritual, emotional, and even mental problems could be resolved among the saints if caring Christians would fully accept their biblical responsibility to show authentic Christian love and concern for their brothers and sisters in the body of Christ. Techniques of group therapy used widely in society today are built on basic principles developed in the early church.

In these perilous, polarized, apocalyptic days, people are looking for any nugget of hope; it is easy to find opportunities to proclaim the acceptable year of the Lord. In fact, it is almost impossible to avoid it! Newspaper headline and television commentaries seem to be designed to instill fear, uneasiness, and uncertainty. This presents an open door for the saints to quiet the hearts of the fearful with a reassuring *word of hope*.

This witness can be accomplished only by Spirit-filled, Spirit-led *mature* believers who are *thoroughly equipped* in *sound* doctrine. Godly spirituality and biblical church growth results from every member of the body fully using his or her spiritual gift or gifts, in submission to the Holy Spirit and in cooperation with other believers (see Colossians 2:19).

Living above the Fray

I will introduce this section with a story I heard at some point in my life. A college professor was chiding one of his students who happen to be a Christian. He poked fun at the Bible speaking about not being able to understand it or get any meaning from it. The student explained to him that he could not understand the Bible first of all because it was not written to him; it is a love letter from God, the Father to His children!

As I write this book I still hear the young man who exclaimed, "It is impossible to live by the standards found in the Bible, so why should I try? You can be sure that if you are reading this and have reached that conclusion, it is none other than Satan. He uses this argument to keep you off balance. The Bible is loaded with God's promises to keep those who are His in perfect peace. He wants us to understand that this love letter from Him only requires our love, trust and obedience. That means that His truths are not open to change. Cultural norms have led many to believe that the Bible is displaced today through the ongoing secular worldview. Daily we see the philosophy of the culture eroding the spiritual life of the church and drawing away many people from the truth of God's Word. The secular view begins with "no God" and "no truth." So church for many has become just another place where I can feel good and have a good time. Actually many are developing their very own ideal of spirituality [life living or style of life] in reference to the things of the Triune God.

Their worship has become a dull, lifeless, and predictable ritual. They display more reverence for their own theology and religious traditions than for biblical truth. They talk about superficial matters; and there is little if any concern or real involvement in each other's lives. Unless we come to comprehend "with all saints," as the apostle Paul says, *[You/we] "may be able to comprehend with all the saints what is the breadth and length and height and depth, and to know the love of Christ which surpasses knowledge; that you may be filled with all the fullness of God" (Ephesians 3:18-19).* Rather than displaying some kind of superficial thinking as did the college professor, an unbeliever, at the beginning of this section, in verse 17, Paul speaks of the requirement that every believer be indwelt by Christ through faith [happens at the moment of salvation] being rooted and grounded in love *established* on the *strong foundation* of giving self and serving love for God and His people (see Matthew 22:37-39; 1 John 4:9-12, 19-21).

If Satan has his way, the types of incidents we are seeing in our society such as the Secret Service incident and incidents among our military and other service organizations will be accepted as the norm even in some local churches. Secular religion wants the church to be reduced to just another service organization under the State. If that happens, it will be because the church has given up and forfeited the battle, which really belongs to God. Having served many years in the military I can say from experience, when discipline and camaraderie are gone you are stuck with a mob.

Mobs don't win battles—they excel at infighting! Satan's secret weapon remains, "spiritual ignorance of God's transforming truth!" The same holds true for the church, it seems that each issue concerning immorality that hits the culture has many allies within the local church where we continue to pound on what is wrong without teaching what is right! Satan is pleased! Every man-made institution has some foundational principles with mandatory basic and advanced training not only in the cognitive realm, but also in hands on performance training. In the church we seem to have some knowledge of what is required of us, but taking proper action creates a problem. Many talk a godly spirituality, but fail to live it out [their talk and walk are not in sync].

REFLECTION

Do not remove the ancient landmark
which your fathers have set.
(Proverbs 22:28)

Review Responses (Chapter 14)

1. The most important thing I learned from this chapter was:

2. The area that I need to work on the most is:

3. I can apply this lesson to my life by:

4. Closing statement of Commitment.

CHAPTER 15

HAVING A HEART FOR OTHERS

I read a story some time ago about a young girl who became the queen of a small country. As she made her initial appearance before her subjects from the balcony of the palace; to her surprise there were hundreds of people on the plaza below cheering her. Very excited, she asked her aunt who had accompanied her, "Does all of those people belong to me?" Her aunt replied, "No darling, you belong to them!" There is a great lesson here for the church (individually and corporately). I ran across this very appropriate poem in my library, by an unknown poet:

OTHERS

Lord, help me to live from day to day
In such a self forgetful way
That even when I kneel to pray
My prayer shall be for others.
Help me in all the work I do
To ever be sincere and true
And know that all I'll do for you
Must needs be done for others.
Let self be crucified and slain
And buried deep—and all in vain

May efforts be to rise again
Unless to live for others.
And when my work on earth is done
And my new work in Heaven begun
May I forget the crown I've won
While thinking still of others.
Others, Lord, others
Let this my motto be,
That I may live like Thee.

Anon

Others (John 3:15-17)

God so loved the world (v. 16) that He gave His only begotten Son to the world. His Son so loved us (v. 15) and gave us of His nature (2 Corinthians 5:17); so that we can love Him by loving others and giving ourselves away in His service. John 3:15 is the first time *eternal life* is mentioned in John's Gospel (see John 3:16; 4:36; 5:39; 6:54, 68; 17:2-3). When a person trusts Christ he or she is born again and receives the Holy Spirit and eternal life [God's kind of spirituality] (v. 17). Praise God! His love is not restricted to any one nation or to *any* spiritual elite. World in this passage probably includes all of creation (see Romans 8:19-22; Colossians 1:20).

Love is an *action* word. People want to see, not hear the rhetoric. You certainly can't tell anybody about the love of God if you don't have the love of God in your heart. That is the love that draws people to Christ. Much of what I have written so far in this book concerns what we; and the churches are *to be [words]* but there is also the element of what we are *to do [deeds]* as well. That combination of preaching and healing was what Jesus modeled: Matthew reports, *"Jesus went about all the cities and villages, teaching in the synagogues, proclaiming the Good News*

of the kingdom, and healing every disease and every sickness"
(see Matthew 9:35). I stated earlier, as Jesus prepared to leave His
disciples, He told them to carry on His mission in the world: *"As
the Father has sent Me, so I send you" (v. 20:21)*.

Jesus our Example

In spite of what some teach, Jesus did not heal the sick simply
to entice people to hear His message. The Scripture bear witness
that Jesus devoted time meeting people's physical needs. Jesus
ministered because He had compassion for hurting people (see
Matthew 14:14; 15:32; 20:34; Mark 1:41). If Jesus is our only
perfect example, then the church today *must* combine *word* and
deed out of compassionate love for the world.

In many ways Jesus, challenged the *status quo* of His time: its
view of women, wealth, power, leadership, and violence. Jesus'
example calls the church to follow Him in pursuing a new vision.
After the resurrection, Jesus sent His indwelling Spirit so that
He could continue to be a transforming presence in the world
through His followers. Just as Jesus took on the form of a servant
(see Philippians 2:7), Christians are to be humble ambassadors of
Christ's healing power and His ministers of reconciliation in being
and doing.

Jesus Commanded

When Jesus sent out the twelve on their first preaching mission, He
commanded them *"to proclaim the kingdom of God and to heal"*
(Luke 9:2). When Jesus sent out the seventy, He commanded them
to *"heal the sick, and tell them, 'the kingdom of God has come to
you" (Luke 10:9)*. His final commands in the Great Commission
in Matthew 28 also point to word and deed. We fulfill the basic
command of making disciples in a two-fold process: by baptizing
those who hear and accept the Gospel and by "teaching them to

obey everything that [Jesus] has commanded you" (v. 20). What did Jesus command His disciples to do? Both to preach and to heal! If Jesus combined word and deed then commanded His followers to do the same, then as His followers we must do the same.

Jesus Preached

If Jesus had defined the gospel only as forgiveness of sins, then we could just invite sinners to accept forgiveness through the cross. Sinners could accept salvation and move on to eternal life at the same time refusing to change any other part of their lives; just live the way that suit them until Jesus come. Jesus said the gospel is the Good News of the kingdom (see Luke 4:43).

Long before He came the prophets had spoken of the future Messiah who would usher in the kingdom of God. Accepting divine forgiveness was the only way of entering the kingdom of God. However, that was not all there was to the kingdom. There was a horizontal relationship with neighbor and especially the poor, broken, and marginal people (see Matthew 11:4-5), as well as the vertical relationship with Christ.

Jesus taught His followers to pray daily, "Your kingdom come. Your will be done on, on earth as it is in heaven" (see Matthew 6:10). His kingdom comes when His will is done on earth. Our sharing of the gospel must present the vertical and horizontal plan of transformation worked by the gospel of Jesus Christ.

Since our Lord's gospel is the Good News of the kingdom, not only forgiveness of sins, but true godly spirituality will combine word and deed (whole person) ministry the way Jesus did. Authentic Christians' godly spirituality will incarnationally engage in God's special concern and care for the poor and marginalized as Jesus did. A godly spirituality will cause biblical Christians to challenge what is wrong in the status quo, as Jesus did; and will preach, teach and live the gospel as He did.

Healing the whole person

Whole person ministry is God's people fleshing out the truth of the gospel outside the four walls. God's love made tangible through basic subsistence such as food, clothing and assistance with everyday living expenses; but whole person ministry also hugs, encourages, challenges and prays for and with the many poor and broken people during the ongoing process of personal transformation.

REFLECTION

The poor man and the oppressor
Have in common:
The LORD gives light to the eyes of
Both. (Proverbs 29:13).

Study Responses (Chapter 15)

1. The most important thing I learned from this chapter was:

2. The area that I need to work on the most is:

3. I can apply this lesson to my life by:

4. Closing statement of Commitment:

CHAPTER 16

COMMUNITY OUTREACH

"But you shall receive power when the Holy Spirit has come upon you; and you shall be witnesses to Me in Jerusalem, and in all Judea and Samaria, and to the end of the earth" (Acts 1:8).

Jesus' restatement of the Great Commission truly impacted my vision for the church during the past 30 years as a pastor and a teacher. Prior to coming into the pastoral ministry in the American church, my wife and I had the opportunity to serve alongside authentic foreign missionaries overseas, some spending their lifetime on the field and others on rotation depending on the policy of their sponsoring denomination or other ministry organization.

Those experiences happened in the Republic of Panama (1970-73) and the Republic of South Korea (1980-82) while assigned to these duty stations (U.S. Army), I was accompanied by my family on each assignment. My wife and I came from Baptist backgrounds, however, during both of these tours we worked with missionaries sponsored by Pentecostal denominations. Our ministry was greatly impacted by those opportunities. Between the traditional churches and the Pentecostal groups, ministry to the whole person seemed to be the focus of both toward the poor and marginalized people. The Pentecostals seemed to be reaching more with the gospel. I'm convinced that's the reason the Pentecostal/ Charismatic groups are reportedly experiencing the fastest-growth worldwide today. Our philosophy of ministry and methods were greatly influenced by these experiences.

Magdalene, and I have been married 49 years; we've been involved in equipping ministry for the past 40 years. We founded the Bread of Life Ministries in 1998 as stated in an earlier chapter. This ministry consists of a non-traditional Bible Institute (1 School in 7 locations) with the express purpose of equipping saints for the work of ministry (see Ephesians 4). A year later we began a network of churches, now at 9, on or near the campuses with the primary mission of nurturing their disciples to maturity and taking the gospel of Christ to the lost people of the world (beginning in their own Jerusalem) per Acts 1:8. "You shall receive power *when* the Holy Spirit has come upon you," ministering to the whole person (physically and spiritually). All of the tenets of the Great Commission [a godly spirituality of preaching, teaching, baptizing, witnessing, and evangelizing the world] hinge on this verse and the Holy Spirit's ministry in and through us and our local church (body).

Jesus' ministry was consumed with the Father and the Holy Spirit; with Him as our Example, how can we settle for any other ministry strategy. I say "any other" because we are faced with some organizations even whole denominations that base their teaching on science, reason, and other natural capabilities without the Holy Spirit. To these folks the Holy Spirit went back to heaven after His work at Pentecost. Many casualties and failed ministries are the result of such teaching. Like Jesus during His earthly ministry, we must be Holy Spirit empowered because we *will be* misunderstood and perceived as the enemy of the status quo. People love the familiar so much that you can read God's instructions to them from the Holy Bible; but because of fear, position, power or other selfish interests many will reject you and the truth you stand for. Stand! My wife and I were licensed and ordained in the Baptist denomination and privileged to pastor churches in that denomination for 28 years. We did not abandon our faith when we founded the Bread of Life Ministries in 1998, to do so would have negatively affected our spiritual foundation (see Jude 3). I highly esteem small group ministry. I gained respect for small group during my early years growing up in our local church. The church had an age-graded Sunday school, various church departments, auxiliaries and clubs. Our church faithfully contributed to missions and was listed in the State Convention's accredited listing annually. However, across the board denominationally, during the latter part of modern times, the local churches across denominational lines seem to have lost its sense of community (love) for all people, even some in the church. So a matter of moving to another denomination or becoming nondenominational is futile without a separate vision from the Lord for a special work. The only accomplishment otherwise would be to transport our misery with us or run into another strain of the same.

Christianity is alive and requires active participation. We often hear, "They are getting the Word, but they are doing nothing with it!" Frequently I am confronted by students who really want to take the ministry of their church into their own hands, so to speak. Many local churches today are operating on a theology of "believe and be baptized." If we are not careful this will lead to an "only Sunday morning crowd mentality." The Great Commission! What is that? Unless we have an outreach to others—why are we here? Ignorance of the truths of God's Word remains one of Satan's most effective and deceptive weapons in his arsenal.

The Local Church

Imagine if you will that you are conversing with an unchurched young man (a student at the Community College) who comes from a family who has never attended church nor participated in any of its activities. He is a good student, but has no knowledge of Christianity or the local church. When you invite him to church, he asks you, "What is the church and please explain its purpose. What would you tell him?

As with many local churches your explanation would probably focus on the experiences and activities that happen [within] the four walls. In most cases *little* if any of your explanation concerns what your church is doing [without] on mission to the world. The fact that God charges each local church to be on mission to the world is the focus of this chapter. Ask people why they chose the church they belong, their response would likely be, the pastor's gifted preaching, music, the quality of their youth group, the friendly welcome or any number of reasons. While all of these are valid reasons, you missed the *primary* reason your church exists and that being to bring converts to maturity and take the gospel of Christ to the world. The Bible declares that, *the first work of the disciples was not preaching, but every-member witnessing.* That remains a part of our charge! It has been said, "The church is what it does; and it does what it is."

In His last discourse with His disciples before His crucifixion, Jesus said to them, *"Ye have not chosen me, but I have chosen you, and ordained you, that ye should go and bring forth fruit, and that your fruit, should remain: that whatsoever ye shall ask of the Father in my name, He may give it you"* (John 15:16). Jesus has called us to be winners, not failures. He expected great things of these first disciples, and they attempted great things for Him. Aren't we His disciples also? I believe today is the day of the saints, now fully restored to the church. We must realize that winning souls is not the occasional business of the church, but its everyday business twelve months a year, as we scatter into the world to live out our godly spirituality.

The church is the body of Christ, and its *primary* mission is to continue what Jesus began to do and to teach. Christ's unique mission was to pay for the sins of humankind with His very life. Thereby He offers a pathway of forgiveness and reconciliation with God. After Jesus accomplished His mission on the cross and God raised Him from the dead, He continued to appear to His followers for forty days. Not only did He prove that He was alive, but He was also giving clear directions on how His disciples are to continue His mission (see v. 3).

America's institutionalized individualism has really hindered the quality and growth of Christ's church in many instances. There is a flurry of individual activities inside and outside of the church wherein people claim to have a special revelation from Christ to do certain activities as His representatives. We must never forget that He is building His church and not on me-ism. Jesus' clear directions can be narrowed down to *four very basic characteristics* derived from the interaction He had with His disciples. He declared that His church would prevail against the gates of hell (see Matthew 16:18 KJV):

1). His church is composed of people who obediently live out their godly spirituality having confessed, Jesus is Lord (see Matthew 16:24-25). I remember as a young person growing up, to most people things were true or false *(no partial or half-truths)*, right or wrong *(no selective disobedience)*. What the Bible said was truth! Today the Bible is still truth! Neither modernism nor postmodernism thought, no matter how sophisticated in appearance or wide spread in communication can change one iota of God's truth. Opinions and (my) private interpretation of God's Word were not a consideration then. People feared God! Today relativism seems to be received among many Christians; so they have begun to observe a hybrid (their own brand wherein he or she determines what is true or false and right or wrong).

2). His church comprises people who live out their spirituality with the threat of Satan and his demons, at the very "gates of hell." Jesus was referring to the spiritual stronghold in which Satan and his legions lurk in the world with the diabolical assignment of destroying the lost, and destroying the testimony of the church. At the same time he is controlling society (his influence increasing daily).

There's no argument, the gates of hell are evident everywhere in our society today. All of our systems (social, judicial, education, and political, etc.) are heavily influenced by the god of this world. It has become vogue to leave God out of all business transactions concerning State, and other secular institutions. It is also politically incorrect to mention Jesus Christ in public. As Christians fail to stand up, this influence has even invaded many local churches through Satan's imbedded decoys.

Imagine a system so secularized that it would offer assistance to a wife only if the husband moves out of the home. Lawyers present their own definition of truth, in order to get the client off. In many cases reaching true truth was never the goal. Several politicians have recently stated that their belief about a particular sin (well noted in both the Old and New Testament as an abomination to God) was evolving. A few days later a few pastors used the same terminology (does biblical truth evolve these days?). It seems that this society wants to view the church as just another social agency under the State; and it seems that more and more pastors are willing to except that place. But know this; the church that Christ is building is counter-cultural and politically incorrect. Why? The reason is biblical. We obey God rather than man. The church's task is to transform the world not be conformed by the world. As more and more local churches withdraw from the public square; Satan roams the streets of any city, U.S.A. challenged by the faithful few only (another misconception accepted as right and the norm); and seeking whom he may devour. The church must confront this foe with Spirit-filled believers who live in obedience to the directions of the Holy Spirit and the Word of God.

3). His church is committed to its Christ given mission. Here meaning it carries out its commitment to the lost of this world [foreign and domestic]. Not only to its task to care for, feed, and protect God's people, but to provide (whole person) ministry to the unsaved through outreach. It is so sad to see how few churches feel, teach, or carry out a passion for the lost. It is an established fact, unless the dual roles of equipping ministry inside and missions outside are equally understood and practiced in the local church, true fruitfulness will be impossible. If we neglect one or the other [half obedience is no obedience]. In Luke 15 we find the passage where Jesus relates the parables of the lost sheep, the lost coin, and the lost son. In the parable of the lost sheep, one sheep, out of a flock of one hundred went astray. The shepherd immediately left the ninety-nine to search for the one lost. Once he found the sheep, he hoisted it upon his shoulder and came home rejoicing. In (v. 7), after countering the Pharisees and scribes Jesus said, *"I say to you that likewise there will be more joy in heaven over one sinner who repents than over ninety-nine just persons who need no repentance."* The scribes and Pharisees felt they did not need to repent because they were not lost.

Through the years we have had numerous people leave our church feeling that their needs as believers had not been met, and seriously speaking, many of them had legitimate complaints. It's like the old proverbial church meeting where the discussion of maintenance of the facility prevents time for discussion of the true spiritual condition of the people. I'm grieved that during most of those years has anyone so much as complained about our ineffectiveness as a mission to the world outside.

Many have left for personal reasons; none have left because we failed to care for lost souls. Has a member of you church left because your church was failing in outreach to the lost? The truth of the matter is that the greatest way to neglect the needs of God's people is to put them in a church that fails to have a functioning outreach to the lost. I have learned through years of discipling men and women that I can teach them the truths and commitments of our faith without seeing any automatic zeal for outreach ministry. When I put them in an environment of outreach, I find them hungry and anxious to be fed and nurtured. Much in the way that eating creates no appetite for exercise, so too I have found that Bible study and prayer alone *do not* create mission-oriented Christians. But, just as exercise creates a desire for food and drink mission-related activities create an insatiable thirst and hunger to feed on God's Word. The *"Down Reach"* of Christ's love that saves people must be channeled through us as an *"Out Reach"* of that love, which brings others into contact with His redemptive provisions.

All churches are **warned**, no matter how successful and efficient the programs may appear on the inside of the walls, so far as the church *fails to bring the gospel to the knowledge of the unsaved by going to the people outside—she disobeys the last command of her Lord, declines in her godly spirituality, forfeits her commission, and risks the removal of her candlestick out of its place (see Revelation 2:5).*

The problem of evangelizing is great because the factors are gigantic, involving on the one hand the whole world of the unsaved, and on the other hand the whole church of the redeemed. In spite of the modern and postmodern thought of many, the church's greatest responsibility of this age is establishing the kingdom of God on earth by the immediate execution of the Lord's marching orders, *"Go make disciples of all nations."*

However, the true church accepts the commission to take on the battle for the souls of lost people. And it is greatly disappointed until lost people are being won to the kingdom of God. We are a supernatural people with a beyond Supernatural God! Give Him praise! Hopefully our local churches will realize the Great Commission requires the enlistment of all the forces of the church for the redemption of the world. We must confess, repent and get on task, which remains two-fold, edification and evangelism—we are now partakers of Christ's divine nature (2 Corinthians 5:17; also see 2 Peter 1:2-4).

- Edification/ Conversion—the spiritual nurture and development of the church, I will expand on this definition in a later section (see Ephesians 4:7-16).

- Evangelism/ Witnessing—one of the major themes of the Bible is the presentation of the Gospel of God in Jesus Christ. So that people are brought through the power of the Holy Spirit to a point of decision. That they will accept Christ as their Lord and Savior. And then serve and follow Him as their Lord in the fellowship of the church in a godly spirituality.

Both are indispensable as the church engages in a mighty "Harvest" which is based on this principle that **Christians must go to all—and all must go!** To realize we are all ministers of reconciliation is part of our salvation commitment (see 2 Corinthians 5:18).

4). The Church of the Living God will win the battle against the gates of hell, the ultimate victory for Christ and His church. Jesus has once and forever sealed the defeat of Satan by His death and resurrection. Whenever, you get a little discouraged turn to the Book of Revelation where the very details of the final battle of the war are recorded. In the main time, God has empowered His church to win the daily skirmishes. He has commissioned His church to fight and has promised her power to guarantee victory. To fully receive all the Lord has in store for us; the church must be a people who do not compromise the faith to the enemy in battle for the souls of lost people.

Edification/ (Church Work) and Evangelism/ (Work of the Church)

We must never get so wrapped up in our church work and other in-house duties that we forget the needs of the lost and believers who have been drawn away; which is the other half of our purpose for existence. The basic meaning of these verses is that saints should seek to bring wandering brothers and sisters back to the Lord. "Convert" means "turn back again" (see Luke 22:32). Oh! How easy it is for a saint to be seduced (to be drawn away) from the truth.

In James 5:19-20, James warns, *"Brethren, if anyone among you wanders from the truth, and someone turns him back, let him know that he who turns a sinner from the error of his way will save a soul from death and cover a multitude of sins."* The church must return to the true faith and counter the ungodly spirituality of those professing believers who have been drawn away. The persons who apostatize from the faith they *once* professed are in grave danger of serious discipline and even death (see Hebrews 5:12-6:9; 10:29; 1 John 2:19).

For example the apostle Paul warns, when believers do not properly judge the holiness of the celebration of Communion, they treat with indifference the Lord Himself—in His life, suffering, and *death* (see 1 Corinthians 11:30). Believers are kept from being consigned to hell, not only by divine decree, but by divine intervention. The Lord chastens His people back to righteous behavior and even sends death to some in the church to remove them before they fall away. *"Now to Him who is able to keep you from falling"* (see Jude 24).

In love we should seek them out and help restore them (see Galatians 6:1). Peter admonishes, *"Above all things have fervent love for one another, for love will cover a multitude of sins (1 Peter 4:8).* This kind of love requires the Christian to put another person's spiritual good ahead of his or her own desires in spite of being treated unkindly, ungraciously, or even with hostility (see 1 Corinthians 13:4-7; Philippians 2:1-4). But we may apply these verses to the lost as well. As we see the return of Christ approaching, the more we need to dedicate ourselves to witnessing and other outreach ministries to the lost world! Christians (individually and corporately) who really believes in the return of Christ cannot help but want to win others.

The apostle Paul placed great value on the spiritual growth of the Christian. We sometimes get over zealous in wanting to get our people out to evangelize, however, like Paul perhaps we should warn and teach them concerning tribulation (see 1Timothy 3:2-4). Many leave too soon! They must be established (see v. 2). The church must take the message of Jesus Christ to the people. The leadership of every church is obligated to challenge every member to share in evangelism. Evangelism flows out a godly spirituality (life).

You will win no more people to Christ and exert no more influence for the Savior than the quality of your spiritual life allows. If you've had a genuine conversion experience and even know how to share it, but fail to develop a godly character that is conformed to the image of Jesus Christ, you will be fruitless and ineffective in personal evangelism. To say it bluntly, you cannot expect to witness successfully while being content with the status quo life. Think of how encouraging it must have been for the disciples when they heard Jesus say, *"You are already clean because of the Word I have spoken unto you" (John 15:3).* We have a couple of peach trees in our backyard, which I prune back to make them produce more fruit. Jesus carefully groomed His apostles for effective service. Above all else, their lives had to be pure.

At the very beginning of His own ministry, Jesus revealed the secret of how to live a pure and victorious life. He told Satan, *"It is written: "Man does not live by bread alone, but by every word that comes out of the mouth of God" (Matthew 4:4; quoted from Deuteronomy 8:3).* So the secret, to our usefulness to God is determined by <u>our daily intake of and yielding to God's Word</u>. The Scriptures are the Source of our spiritual strength. They build a godly spirituality (character) that meets the lifelong prerequisite for effective witness.

Learning to live in obedience to God's will as revealed through His Word is key to experiencing an abundant personal witnessing ministry. We know this because obedience was what mattered most with Jesus during His earthly life. To be fully effective in evangelism, you must emulate Jesus in His willingness to please the Father. Obedience to His leadership must become your continual and highest goal in life. This begins slowly and grows through wholehearted allegiance to God's Word.

We live in a day when a friendly smile with many people is considered suspect. People are so uptight and fearful these days that they think it will cost them something to even be neighborly. This ploy of Satan has unbalanced many believers and they react in the same manner as the unsaved person. Every Christian must overcome this obstacle and we can by realizing that God is the Source of our witness. Jesus, our Example, spoke of that Source, *"The words I speak to you are not just My own, rather, it is the Father, living in Me, who is doing His work" (John 14:10).*

Satan strives to unravel the believer to the point that he or she doesn't want to get involved with the poor and marginal people because, "They think the person will just rip them off!" This person is not reflecting the true Source; and I'm sure he or she is grieving the Spirit. Satan knows that your friendliness will allow people to identify with you in a natural way. People are attracted to those who know how to laugh, sing, and engage in athletics, the arts, and just enjoy being *real*.

I believe that the year 2000 marked a turning point in the restoration of the church. Further, I believe that just as the Holy Spirit returned the five ministers of Ephesians 4:11, in years past so beginning in 2000 the true Spirit-filled saints, [those who follow in the footsteps of Jesus, with the goal of pouring themselves out sacrificially for others] are returned to the church. Christ sent us to convert the world, not to be conformed to it. These people are taking upon themselves the solemn responsibility of telling men and women the joyful news that Christ died on Calvary to save them from their sins.

Every year the crime rate goes up and the average age of criminals comes down. Dishonesty in the board room, politics, national and local governments, employer-employee relationships has reached gigantic proportions. Murders, thefts, cyber-crimes, vandalism, alcoholism, drug addictions, sexual perversities, adult and child abuse give rise to more victims each day.

One of the most striking elements in this darkness is the failure of many people even some Christians to be shocked or alarmed when these disclosures hit the media. One deterrent to check this overwhelming flood tide of evil is through personal evangelism. The spread of the Christian faith can be a major obstacle to these forces of evil that are undermining the character of every institution upon which this nation was founded. One thing is sure we are beyond debate, so why not return to the truths of God's Word? Our offensive weapon as soldiers of the cross remains the Word of God. The Word is the Sword of the Spirit. This is standard equipment for waging a successful battle in gaining a constituency for Christ. The Sword can pierce the conscience and penetrate the soul with radical effects.

The glaring failures in our national institutions are forcing people to be fearful and doubt the uncertainties of things in our society that a few years ago were taken for granted. However, I believe today is a greater time of opportunity for the Church of Jesus Christ! Humanity is rushing headlong to the only alternative, Jesus Christ, "the Answer!" This brings into focus the Biblical declaration that He has the name far above *"every name that is named, not only in this world, but also in that which is to come"* *(see Ephesians 1:21).*

- Name the problem and He is above it.
- Name the crisis and He is above it.
- Name the emergency and He is above it.
- He is the only name that is adequate for every need.

Since Christ is the only "center of gravity" in the spiritual universe, His church is faced with the responsibility [great privilege] of bringing within His sphere of influence those who would be hopelessly lost. The particularity of the message declares that there is only one open Door to salvation. The saints point out and lead the lost to the Door, Jesus Christ.

When the Bible is proclaimed, it discloses the source of sin; it exposes the deceitfulness of the human heart; and proposes a total remedy for sin through Christ's redemptive acts of reconciliation. Kindness fought with the weapons of the Word, prayer and divine love is our defense. When the moral structure crumbles from the inside of any institution, nation, family or government it becomes easy prey to the enemy outside. When evangelism which is the reproductive power of the church ceases to function, the church becomes sterile and decadent; it becomes indifferent to the spiritual needs of its constituency; it loses its sense of mission in the world; and its worship turns into a meaningless routine.

When Christians are lazy and fail to evangelize, the very existence of the church is threatened! Remember, nothing can match the awesome power of God, who responds to the church's call for help in the day of battle. The problem is not God's refusal to give grace but rather the church's refusal to ask God for the strength to stand Satan's onslaught. In the garden of Gethsemane, Jesus warned his disciples, as He still warns us, against the laziness and inattentiveness that leads to the danger.

"Watch and pray
so that you will not fall into temptation.
The spirit is willing, but the flesh is weak"
(Matthew 26:41).

Certainly the church will have her struggles and even some failures; but Christ, the Owner of the church has declared that even the gates of hell cannot stand against her.

Remember, too, that the teaching and miracles of Jesus Himself did not convert most of Jerusalem. Our task is not to think as if God needs help to build His church. If we just be faithful in delivering the message; God will take care of the results. Notice how the apostle Paul described his own ministry:

"For we are to God the fragrance of Christ
among those who are being saved
and among those who are perishing.
To the one we are aroma of death leading to death,
and to the other the aroma of life leading to life.
And who is sufficient for these things?"
(2 Corinthians 2:15-16)

Paul emphasizes the twofold effect of the gospel. To some, the message brings eternal life and ultimately glorification. To others, it is a stumbling block of offense that brings eternal death. He further points out that no one in his own strength is adequate or competent to serve God in the ways that he had been describing. Any ministry that is faithful to God will reap a harvest; it will also confront the mocking rejection of the multitude.

Christ's church will be victorious! Christ's church will see large numbers of lost people won to Christ and well integrated into the family of God. Through the church, God's kingdom comes and His will is done on the earth! Give Him praise and glory!

REFLECTION

Do not speak in the hearing of a fool
for he will despise the wisdom of your words
(Proverbs 23:9).

Study Responses (Chapter 16)

1. The most important thing I learned from this chapter was:

2. The area that I need to work on the most is:

3. I can apply this lesson to my life by:

4. Closing statement of Commitment:

CHAPTER 17

EFFECTIVE EVANGELISM

*And the things that you have heard from me among
many witnesses, commit these to faithful men who will
be able to teach others (2 Timothy 2:2).*

A major problem of this new generation seems to be a desire to
do away with all vestiges of the prior generation's church. This is
not necessarily bad. There's a *difference* between what a church
believes and what it practices. *The church's faith must **not change**,
because it is based on the eternal, absolute truth of the Bible. The
church's practices [how the church implements its faith], however,
must change from generation to generation as well as from culture
to culture **if the church is to be relevant**, that is, to communicate the
gospel clearly to new generations so that they at least understand
the message.* If a church desires to reach its generation in the
culture, it must adapt its practices [**not its faith**] to that culture.
This is one of the most important principles that the church of the
twentieth century missed. When my family and I arrived in Panama
in 1970, one of the first things I noticed in the churches was the
great attempt to acculturate the people in traditions, beliefs and
practices [to include music, dress, and hairstyles] of the foreign
denominational planters. The churches even had foreigners for
pastors. Immediately, I could see and feel the animosity among

the indigenous ministers. Certainly this mistrust and resentment formed from the old colonial image even found in the church. However, the church went through tremendous change over the next decade. I was acquainted with pastors who were native born in Central and South America who returned home when the door opened for them to assume the pastorate of their native churches. Several of these pastors that I was acquainted with there, were experienced pastors of churches here in the U.S. for years prior to this great move of God upon the church to include indigenous pastors. The records of the results of this move around the world stand for themselves.

The churches in America had access to the move of the Spirit as early as the 1906 [Azusa Revival], however, because of rejection as a result of tradition, customs, and other reasons, the churches have fared poorly at the end of the century and at the beginning of the twenty-first century. As a teacher, I receive many complaints and honest inquires from pastors and congregants concerning the great exodus from the traditional churches of all denominations. I hear comments like, "the Word is preached but the people won't listen or apply it." Then some of the people claim, "The message is not relevant for today, etc."

The culture at large in this country has rejected the message of Christ; but I think more than rejection of the gospel; it's a rejection of the church's outdated, culturally irrelevant methods, customs and traditions passed down from the founders have kindled the rejection of both the gospel and the church (see 1 Corinthians 1:2,3). Over the years, established churches build up a number of customs, practices, and traditions that has become set in concrete. That's because these practices have proved valuable and helpful in the past. In the present, however, they are "excess baggage," because times change and so must our practices and traditions. But in far too many of these churches, the need for change is never realized. Jesus indicates that it is hard to change established traditions (see Matthew 9:16-17). In this passage Jesus is not evaluating those practices or saying that one is better than the other. He's warning of the difficulties for those who attempt to bring change into situations where structures are already in place. The advantage of change is that people who are attracted come into a new situation in which they're open to ejecting much of their old "baggage."

Over the past fifty years or so, Christ has fully restored the five ministers of Ephesians 4 and the Spiritual gifts of Romans 12; 1 Corinthians 12, and those found in various other passages. Even though there is much resistance to change, abuse with titles and gift confusion, the local churches could make a much better response to the world's search and cry for spirituality, by shaking off their excess baggage and returning to the Bible-based, Spirit-filled Community of love; that Jesus is building through the Holy Spirit's ministry in those local churches, which are open to Him (see Matthew 16:18).

I've noticed through my studies of church history, that during the last half of the nineteenth century, the mark of the church was holiness. In the early twentieth century the mark was the baptism of the Holy Spirit with tongues. The latter half of the twentieth century saw the restoration of the five-fold body gifts and the Spiritual gifts operating among the laity with emphasis on the ministry of the Holy Spirit in the body of Christ [the Church]. The Holy Spirit has returned to the church after an eleven century absence. In fact, on April 6, 2006, many churches and Christians marked the centennial through special services and celebrations in many countries of the world.

We find ourselves here beginning the second decade of the twenty-first century and it seems we are determined [even though the leadership is aware of this great move of God] to give Satan a free hand in the churches through the mentality that the state is a higher authority than God Himself. We go into Sunday services, hear the messages and teaching then disconnect and return to our religiosity under the dictation of the state until next Sunday for more churchanity. Satan in the meantime is seemingly going unnoticed and continues his ferocious attack on the foundations, and with the termite's precision tearing down or redefining the institutions this nation was founded upon [under Almighty God] including the power and influence of the church. That is, the church that humankind is building with its ungodly spirituality (see Revelation 3:16). Some of the countries that were missionized by this and other great nations are today sending their missionaries to America seemingly to bring us back to God!

What a turn-a-bout! We are confronted by humanism. Marriage is being re-defined and no longer to be only between one man and one woman. In spite of the fact that any alternative is a recorded abomination to God in both the Old and New Testament (see Leviticus 18:22; 20:13; Romans 1:27; 1 Corinthians 6:9; 1 Timothy 1:10; Genesis 19:1-29). We need a revival, an outpouring of the Holy Spirit.

One major hindrance to the Holy Spirit's work in the local churches flows from the secularization of much of the materials and programs used in Christian education; which equates to natural abilities. The churches conduct renewal conferences to insure that constitutions, by-laws, and church covenants are relevant with the culture. However very few think it's worth equal time to come together as God's people to see if we are still in "the faith" of Jude 3.

God loves us, and it is His will to work through us. Certainly we know that within ourselves, alone we cannot lead anyone to Christ; but the Holy Spirit is faithful to do so through us. Jesus said, "And when He is come, He will convict the world of sin, of righteousness and of judgment; of sin, because they do not believe in Me; of righteousness, because I go to the Father and you see Me no more; of judgment because the ruler of this world is judged" (John 16:8-11).

Therefore, when we are yielded, our evangelism task becomes totally automatic in the godly lives of believers because of the indwelling presence of the Holy Spirit of God. *"It is God who works in you both to will and to do His good pleasure" (Philippians 2:13).*

Character is a Choice

If you are going to be used of God, it is imperative that you come to a place of victory in your own personal holiness (purity). Temptation comes in many ways to everyone who works in the kingdom of God. Satan wants to destroy the testimony of Christians, so he tries to draw them away and tempt them to compromise with sin. His intent is to produce the continual presence of guilt in our lives. Praise God! Christ has given us His full and effective victory in this matter.

The Scripture promises, "If we confess our sins, He is faithful and just to forgive us our sins and to cleanse us from all unrighteousness" (1 John 1:9). Because temptations will come you need to understand that your holiness of thought and singleness of purpose are extremely pleasing to God. Your holiness (purity) is not determined for you. It requires a personal choice on your part. Notice what the apostle Paul wrote to the young pastor Timothy: *"But in a great house there are not only vessels of gold and silver, but also of wood and clay, some for honor and some for dishonor. Therefore if anyone cleanses himself from the latter, he will be a vessel for honor, sanctified and useful for the Master, prepared for every good work"* (2 Timothy 2:20-21). In this "great house" analogy, Paul contrasts two kinds of utensils or serving bowls: (1) some for honor—in a wealthy home, the ones made of precious *"gold and silver"* were used for honorable purposes such as serving food to the family and their guests. (2) some for dishonor—those made of *"wood and clay"* were not for any honorable use, but rather those uses which were repulsive such as disposing of garbage and other household waste.

Paul is explaining to Timothy that there are four levels of witnessing or ministry that we can experience as believers. We can *choose* to be vessels of gold, silver, wood, or clay. Again, the choice is yours! Verse 21 says, *"if anyone cleanses himself,"* in other words whoever wants to be useful to the Lord for His glorious purposes; even a *wooden bucket* or a *clay pot* becomes useful when purged and made holy (pure). I must clean myself. If a person cleanses themself from these things, they can be used:

- Abstain from godless conversations (v. 16)
- Wickedness (v. 19)
- Lustful desires (v. 22)
- Foolish arguments (v. 23)

Notice all of these sins are the *choices* of the individual having to do with purity (holiness). Once he or she cleanses themself; by *choosing* to be clean, that individual will be like gold or silver. Verse 19 tells us, *"The solid foundation of God stands, having this seal:"*

- The Lord knows those who are His.
- They have departed from iniquity.

Paul gives these two characteristics of those with the divine seal of authenticity and shows God's ownership of believers, which is their pursuit of holiness (see 1 Corinthians 6:19, 20; 1 Peter 1:15, 16). This is likely a reference to the church (see 1 Timothy 3:15), which cannot be overcome by the gates of hell (see Matthew 16:18) and is made up of those who belongs to Him. Tragically, many Christians and churches settle for being drab-looking pottery:

- They never have an effective testimony.
- They never learn the Word of God.
- They never choose a life of uncompromising moral and ethical standards for living a godly spirituality.

Because of their failure to strive to be vessels of gold, they fail to lead others to Christ and make little or no impact on family, friends or community. Christ never ordained that a Christian be mediocre or half-hearted; or that he or she be undisciplined, unloving, or un-joyful. Actually, Jesus came to give us life and to give it to us abundantly (see John 10:10). Another reality that causes many Christians to be ship-wrecked is their allowing the old nature to rise up and dominate the new nature. I read a story of a man who had two fighting dogs, one black and one gray, each Saturday afternoon he took the dogs to the village to fight; at the same time taking bets on which dog would win. The one he chose won every time. A man inquired of him how it was possible for him to know which dog would win. He told him the one I feed the most always wins. Our two natures are locked in conflict with each other. In daily experiences it is a known fact that the nature you feed will win every time.

You may be a dedicated, blood-washed Christian and even be the head of a special ministry, but one thing is certain, the nature you feed, the old nature or the new nature is the one that will become stronger and dominate the other. In order to *cleanse yourself every day,* you will have to crucify [starve] your old nature and feed your new nature:

- with the Word of God
- with spiritual praise
- with prayer
- with the fellowship of growing Christians

The key is feeding the new nature on the Word of God meditating upon it daily during your quit time; then by obeying the Scriptures through practical application. This will develop gold and silver character qualities in your life (godly spirituality). Recently a local hospital was in hot water for using instruments that were not properly cleaned or sterilized. They can use instruments that are bent, crooked, old or new, *but they can never use dirty instruments!* No matter how new and beautiful they may be. That same truth applies to the Christian life. The only person God *cannot* and *will not* use is one who has a dirty life (ungodly spirituality). He can use us in spite of:

- our ignorance
- our personality defects
- our idiosyncrasies

But He will not use a life characterized by impurity (ungodly spirituality) until it is cleansed. If you desire to be used of God:

- As a minister of reconciliation (evangelism).
- As a godly man or woman (edification).
- As you chose to be pure (holy).
- As you plan to succeed in your ministry (service).

If you trust Him to accomplish it through you, then know, right now, you will have victory. *"The one who calls you is faithful and he will do it" (1 Thessalonians 5:24).*

The Importance of the Word of God

It is impossible for a Christian to have a strong evangelistic ministry or be a trainer of disciples without having a very good working knowledge of the Word of God. Satan will oppose your striving and make sure that it does not come easy. It takes great dedication to be in the Scriptures on a daily basis. In the Bible, we have all we need for a life of godliness. The writings of teachers and preachers help us to better understand the Word of God; but it's so important to remember—only the Bible, the Word of God can impart life to our souls. Paul wrote in Colossians 2:6, *"As you therefore have received Christ Jesus the Lord, so walk in Him, rooted and built up in Him and established in the faith, as you have been taught, abounding in it with thanksgiving."* He encouraged them and us to continue walking with Christ. As you were saved by faith, so walk by faith. Notice the four expressions to describe the Colossians' walk with Christ:

- Rooted
- Built up
- Established
- Abounding

The tense of the word "rooted" denotes a completed action (maturity); the believers have been rooted in Christ. The next three words "built up," "established," and "abounding," are in the present tense, showing the continual growth that should characterize every Christian's walk with Christ.

Conversational Evangelism

> *"Beware lest anyone cheat you through philosophy and empty deceit, according to the tradition of men, according to the basic principles of the world, and not according to Christ" (Colossians 2:8).*

There are those who would use this verse to discourage Christians from the study or even reading of philosophy. However, Paul the inspired writer of this verse was adept at philosophy, as evidenced by his interaction with the Stoic and Epicurean philosophers in Athens (see Acts 17:1-34).

Paul was warning the believers not to be taken in by any philosopher that does not conform to a proper knowledge of Christ. The false teachers at Colosse had combined worldly philosophies with the gospel seeking to impose them on believers (sound familiar?). Paul's strongest indictment against these heretics was that their teaching was **not according to Christ,** and thus they were not walking with Christ.

Obviously, our society differs significantly from that of first-century Colosse in many ways. Yet, like the culture of the Roman Empire two millennia ago, our culture is ripe and well-positioned for the message of hope that Jesus commanded us to share in bold and unapologetic ways.

The apostle Paul, the world's first great itinerant evangelist, provided us with the conversational principle, drawn from the example of Jesus' ministry, for effectively communicating the gospel. He admonished the believers in the church of Corinth to contextualize the message—that is, to share the gospel with a culture so that it could understand without compromising or reshaping the work of Christ (see 1 Corinthians 9:19-23). Paul understood that he was called [as we are] to be a faithful messenger of a *timeless message* and that the message itself *would be relevant to all people* in all walks of life, knowing that the manner in which the information was proclaimed might have to shift from one cultural context to another.

Evangelistic Wisdom from the First Century Church

Let's consider a few of the tenets of evangelism prepared for us two millennia ago and put in the Bible. These principles are just as pertinent for us as they were for Peter, James, and John, and all of the other members of that unlikely band who followed Jesus and then turned the world upside down:

- The gospel message belongs to God's story.
- The means of getting the message to those who need to hear it is by people communicating that message through words and actions that are consistent with the truths of God's Word.
- God has and will use any born again person who is open to serving Him to convey the gospel. He will bless the efforts of His servants.
- The most powerful attraction to a nonbeliever is seeing the life of someone transformed by the reality of the gospel. A verbal proclamation without a godly spirituality (lifestyle) to support the proclamation is useless to the witness of the kingdom of God.

- The most effective evangelists are the most obedient and committed Christians. They may not have formal theological training, a position in church, or credentials such as license or ordination. They need a passion for Christ, a desire to make Him known in the world and the boldness and willingness to be used in any way and all situations to help usher others into the kingdom of God.

- We cannot give away what we don't possess. Therefore, we must be in close relationship with God and must be open to being used by Him as a conduit of His grace to others.

- Every Christian must be ready at all times and in all situations to share his or her testimony and the gospel of Christ with those who do not have a relationship with Christ.

- The most effective witnessing efforts are those that are simple and sincere.

- Effective outreach always involves sincere and fervent prayer that God will bless those efforts, although there is no guarantee of the nonbeliever making the right choices.

- Effective evangelism is the *bridge* we build between our love for God and our love for others.

Knowing God's Story

No human words or human ability is capable of describing the price God chose to pay to make salvation possible for us. Meditate on the fact that God Himself died to assure it. "God so loved the world that He gave His only begotten Son, that whoever believes on Him should not perish but have everlasting life" (John 3:16). God's love is not limited to any one person or group of people. World in this verse means all of God's creation. Praise God!

Jesus came so that the world through Him might be saved. There are multitudes of people in the world today who are held hostage by the devil in their minds. First John 3:8 says, ". . . . For this purpose the Son of God was manifested, that He might destroy the works of the devil." Will you accept Him as your Savior, today? When Christ comes again, He will come in judgment upon those who refused *His sacrificial offer* of salvation. To believe the gospel is to receive life and avoid judgment (vv. 15, 16). A person who does not believe not only misses life, but is already condemned (vv. 17, 18). In John 1:12-13, we read, *"But as many as received Him to them He gave the right to become children of God, to those who believe in His name: who were born, not of blood, nor of the will of the flesh, nor of the will of man, but of God."* Each person must individually trust Jesus Christ for eternal life it is a gift to be received (see John 4:10, 14):

- Christ, not religion,
- Christ, not world religious leaders,
- Christ, not a reward achieved through any human effort.

He stands out alone as humankinds' *single* Source of salvation. *"The Word became flesh . . . ." (see v. 14).* The Son of God who was from eternity became human, with limitations in time and space (see Philippians 2:5-8). This is the doctrine of the incarnation: God became human, but lost none of His essential nature of deity. John uses the word "flesh" here referring to the physical nature of humans, not our sinful disposition (contrast Romans 8:1-11). This is God's story! Christ was the Father's single and all-sufficient plan "A" of salvation and redemption for humankind; and there is no plan "B."

Therefore, we can readily see that sharing God's plan of salvation is sharing a person; whose very name, Jesus Christ, explains His divine mission. *"It pleased the Father that in Him all the fullness should dwell, and by Him to reconcile all things to Himself, by Him, whether things on earth or things in heaven, having made peace through the blood of His cross" (Colossians 1:19-20).*

Our motto at the Bread of Life Bible Institute is "Come Learn—Go Teach" our text being 2 Timothy 2:2: *"And the things that you have heard from me among many witnesses, commit these to faithful men who will be able to teach others also."* Timothy was to take the divine revelation he had learned from Paul and teach it to other faithful individuals—people with proven spiritual character and giftedness, which would in turn pass on those truths to the next generation. From Paul to Timothy to faithful men to others encompasses 4 generations of godly leaders. That process of spiritual reproduction, which began in the early church is time-tested and expected to continue until the Lord returns.

As you teach others to share a Word of truth and to give their personal testimony, you must also teach them to present God's plan of salvation in a systematic manner. The overall objective is a disciple (a learner) who is able to guide a person through the Scriptures so that he or she can understand *how* to become a Christian. We are surrounded by a sea of need. People everywhere are hungry for Jesus Christ and for salvation; they're searching for God, but often in this anti-Christian society, have no idea who or what they are looking for. Like the early church, we must be both available and spiritually—prepared; the results will be significant conversions. Rejoice!

Knowing Christ Personally

Jesus Christ is not only concerned with getting people to turn to Him; He wants them to have a conversion experience. This means you have to know how to lead others to an intelligent and Spirit-led decision. A person cannot just conjure up a relationship with Jesus Christ. It is imperative that there be a moment when he or she says, "Yes Jesus! I receive You as my own Lord and Savior." A person must know that he or she is a Christian; know and not guess. One of the best ways you can help people have this settled assurance is through an illustration that a godly man helped me with many years ago and I've found it to be very helpful, called the Gap Illustration, I usually begin by asking two questions which gently opens the door for explaining the illustration:

- What is God like? Usually the answer is: "He is holy" or "He is good" etc.
- What is man like? Usually the answer is: "He is sinful" or "He is bad" etc.

The Gap Illustration

Let's begin with you engaging someone who is interested and eager to listen. Get a sheet of paper (my teacher used a napkin) and write on it: "MAN" and "GOD," then under God write Holy; under man write sinful (**Figure 1 below**). Explain that man has always wanted to know God and in a variety of ways has sought to worship Him." Share with him or her that there is a serious problem that keeps us apart; as reflected in their answers to the two questions above. In Romans 3:23, the Bible tells us what that problem is *"For all have sinned and fall short of the glory of God."*

Hand the person a Bible, point to that verse, and ask him or her to read it aloud. [It's also a great idea for you to learn to read upside down, just in case]. In this anti-Christian society, people are not interested in hearing your opinion about Jesus Christ. Let the Bible do the talking.

After the person has read the verse, carry on a conversation for example: "Joe that verse you have just read says all have sinned. What is it saying about you? Do you identify with that *all.*"

MAN	**GOD**
Sinful	Holy

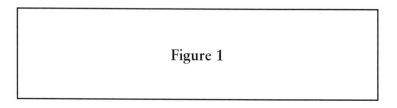

Figure 1

"Yes, I'm a part of that *all*."

"Well, what does that say about you?"

"It says I have sinned."

Joe, "Fallen short of the glory of God' means living a life that is imperfect. All of us have lived lives that are sinful and unlike that of Jesus Christ. His life was sinless and perfect, and all in the world has fallen short of that standard." I've observed that this comparison brings them to understand that they fall short.

Write the reference "Romans 3:23 under "MAN," and write "All have sinned" next to it.

Then draw in the gap between "MAN" and "GOD" and write "SIN" in the space. (**Figure 2**).

MAN	**GOD**
Sinful	Holy

Romans 3:23 "All have sinned"

FIGURE #2

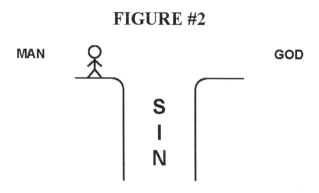

Now turn to Romans 6:23 and have him or her read the verse aloud. *"For the wages of sin is death; but the gift of God is eternal life in Christ Jesus our Lord."* The word "wages" needs some explanation. "Joe, have you ever worked for wages?" He replies, "Yes, I have a job. It's what you get every payday."

"The Bible says sin earns death. When payday comes you will have earned death!" When a person sins and is separated from God, he or she is dead toward God and has no relationship with the Creator. Since all have sinned, and you have sinned, you have earned spiritual death."

"Joe, two kinds of death is explained in the Bible. One is physical, which we're going to look at in a moment, and the other is spiritual, which the Bible is talking about here." At this point pause to write down Romans 6:23 in your illustration and the words, "Sin Earns Death" next to it (**Figure 3**).

MAN   **GOD**

Sinful   Holy

Rom. 3:23-All have sinned
Rom. 6:23-Sin earns death

FIGURE #3

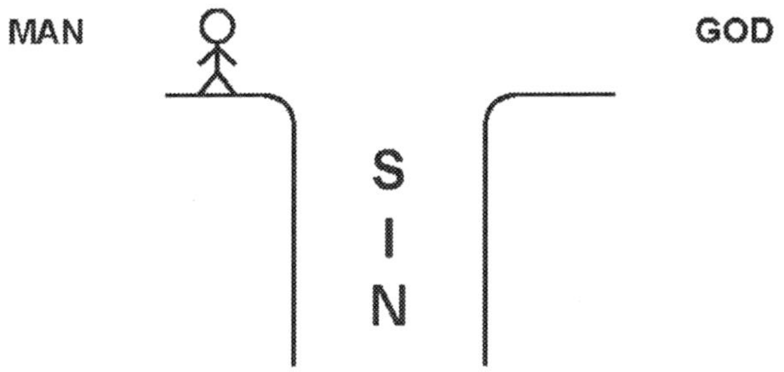

Next, turn to Hebrews 9:27 and let him or her read aloud, *"And as it is appointed for men to die once, but after this the judgment."* Say, "This verse speaks of physical death. God has appointed a time when every man, woman, boy and girl will die physically. Our brief time on earth is to prepare for that all-important day. Only God knows when it will come.

"Joe, some day you're going to die, and so will I. After that we will face God's judgment. When we check the facts, humankind has a real problem that equals eternal death.

Now write "Hebrews 9:27" under the verses with the notation "All die physically" by it. Then summarize the results of these three verses in the words "Eternal Death" (**Figure 4**). You have clearly shown Joe his condition.

MAN   **GOD**

Sinful   Holy

Rom. 3:23-all have sinned
Rom. 6:23-Sin earns death
Heb. 9:27-All die physically

ETERNAL DEATH

FIGURE #4

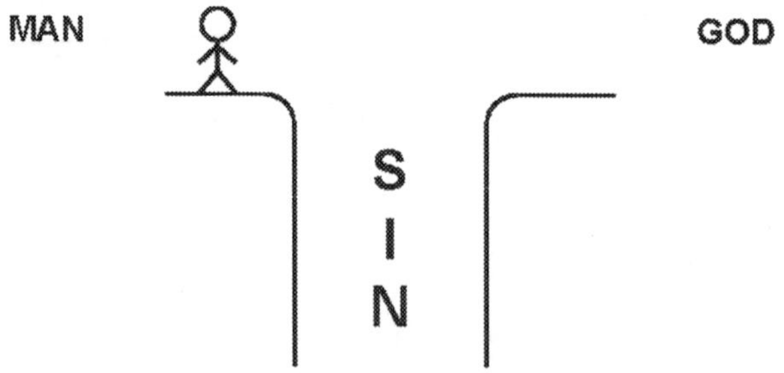

Now you will be able to help him see the wonderful plan made possible by Christ's love. Begin with Romans 5:8, "*While we were still sinners, Christ died for us.*" Joe, you are in the midst of your sins, Christ loves you just as you are.

On the right side of your illustration under "God" write Romans 5:8 and by it the words "Christ died for us while we were still sinners." Now draw a cross bridging the gap between "God" and "Man" (**Figure 5**). This is the reason Jesus went to the cross: to pay the penalty of our sins, so mark through the word "sin."

MAN   GOD

Sinful   Holy

Rom. 3:23-All have sinned   Rom. 5:8 Christ died for
Rom. 6:23-Sin earns death   us while we were still
Heb. 9:27-all die physically   sinners

ETERNAL DEATH

FIGURE #5

MAN   GOD

Now, turn to Ephesians 2:8, 9 *"For it is by grace you have been saved, through faith, and this is not of yourselves, it is the gift of God, not by works, so that none can boast."* "Joe, it is by God's grace and love you don't deserve and a love you never earned. Salvation is strictly a gift." Write "Ephesians 2:8-9 on the right side and by the words "By God's love we are saved through faith" (**Figure 6**). Next turn to John 1:12 and ask your friend to read this verse to you. *"But as many as received Him, to them He gave the right to become children of God, to those who believe* *in His name."* Pay attention to the **two key words** [*believe* and *receive*].

Now say, "Joe, there are *two steps* in this verse that explain how to become a child of God. **The 1ˢᵗ step** is to *believe* in Jesus Christ. You must believe He is who He claimed to be (see Romans 10:9-10). Do you believe that He was born of a virgin; that He lived a sinless life; and He died for your sins; that He arose from the grave on the third day? If you do, take **the 2ⁿᵈ step** which is to *receive* Him as your own Savior and Lord!"

MAN	GOD
Sinful	Holy

Rom. 3:23-All have sinned   Rom. 5:8-Christ died us while
Rom. 6:23-Sin earns DEATH   we were still sinners.
                                 Eph. 2:8-9-By God's love
                                 we are saved through faith

ETERNAL DEATH

FIGURE #6

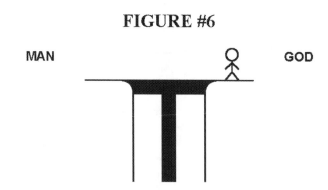

In the final analysis, you are leading Joe to see that Jesus is God and He died for the sins of the whole world; that he must believe that includes him. His believing and receiving this fact by faith must occur for the *rebirth* to be experienced. At this point draw a bridge across the top of the cross on your diagram, and write "Believe and Receive" and "John 1:12" over the top of the bridge; also write "Eternal Life" on the right side (**Figure 7**).

MAN	GOD
Sinful	Holy

Rom. 3:23-All have sinned	Rom. 5:8 Christ died for
Rom. 6:23-Sin earns DEATH	
us while we were still sinners	
Heb. 9:27-All die physically	Eph. 2:8-9-By God's Love
	we are saved through Faith

ETERNAL DEATH   **ETERNAL LIFE**

FIGURE #7

The Assurance of Salvation

And this is the testimony: that God has given us eternal life, and that life is in His Son. He who has the Son has life; he who does not have the Son of God does not have life.

These things I have written to you who believe in the name of the Son of God, that you may know that you have eternal life, and that you may continue to believe in the name of the Son of God (1 John 5:11-13).

We find in these words that the foundation of our assurance of salvation, His Son, of whom the Spirit and the Scripture testify (vv. 11-12). Those who trust Christ can know they have eternal life because God says they have it. The Christian's assurance is not a matter of "working up" a religious emotion; it is simply a matter of taking God at His Word. We note in these verses that eternal life is in Jesus Christ *only* and this is the great truth the Father, the Son, and the Holy Spirit, the water and the blood testify of. Every true Christian has a personal witness from God to his or her faith (see Romans 8:14-16; Galatians 5:6; 2 Corinthians 5:16-17).

The next step is to realize that the church has been put on earth by God to turn people to walk with Him. As a part of the church our place can be seen through a beautiful Bible image. Repeatedly the Bible pictures our purpose on earth as learning to walk with God. *"Enoch walked with God; and he was not; for God took him" (Genesis 5:24). "As you have therefore received Christ Jesus the Lord, so walk in Him" (Colossians 2:6). "They shall walk with Me" (Revelation 3:4).*

Each year as we walk more closely with God, in our doing and our thinking, we become ready, like Enoch, to go on with Him into eternity as with a friend whom we have come to love and trust. Individually and corporately our goal is to bring people through Jesus Christ, to walk with God. With that said, you don't have to evangelize the way of such a great evangelist as Billy Graham. God created each of us to be unique, and that quality encompasses the way we communicate our faith to others. If you are hindered by a lack of focus on others since they haven't dedicated their lives to Christ as you have done, read about God's wrath to better understand what may happen to your friends, loved ones and others (see Luke 16:19-31; Revelation 20:10-15).

The issues at hand are our priorities and our commitment to God and to others. Collectively, our determination in the local church must be to prioritize Christ in our lives by making Him real in the lives of others; and also we personally *become* an irrefutable statement about our faith (Jude 3), and the nature of our hearts.

As we noted earlier, evangelism or any other task for God that is pursued without the benefit of extensive and intensive prayer support is crippled. Unless we call upon God through prayer, we are seeking to do His work in our own strength even though we are unable to complete the task. It makes absolutely no sense to take on this gigantic challenge without the power of God.

Scripture tells us that we are to devote ourselves to prayer, knowing that God hears the prayers of His people and that He responds to our requests. We are told that we don't get the things we desire because we do not pray; and because we do not ask for the right things from God.

We are assured that when we are praying for the salvation of others, God will hear those prayers and is pleased by them. Again, prayer is our power source. Without prayer, we needlessly limit our ability to affect the souls of humankind (see Proverbs 15:8, 29; Colossians 4:2; James 4:2, 3; 5:16).

As you think about the people with whom you are acquainted who do not have Christ in their lives, ask God to change their hearts. Intercede with God to use you as His minister of reconciliation with those people. Beseech Him to include them in the family of faith. God cares about these people, just as He cares for you and me. When we pray for their salvation and are accessible to God as the instrument of grace needed to bring them to Him, we are true servants. It is the power of prayer that facilitates the salvation of spiritually needy friends.

REFLECTION

The fear of the Lord is the beginning of wisdom,
And the knowledge of the Holy
One is understanding. (Proverbs 9:10).

Study Responses (Chapter 17)

1. The most important thing I learned from this chapter was:

2. The area that I need to work on the most is:

3. I can apply this lesson to my life by:

    Closing statement of Commitment:

CHAPTER 18

CARING FOR NEW MEMBERS

"God began doing a good work in you,
I am sure He will continue it until
it is finished when Jesus comes."
(Philippians 1:6 NCV).

One of the most encouraging features of evangelism during these anti-Christian times is the increased attention it is giving to better ways of receiving, training, and conserving those who join the church.

- The most important part of evangelism comes after the decisions have been made and that is conservation.
- The greatest weakness of the evangelism of the past was that it stopped too soon, right (after baptism). However we must fairly take under consideration the help provided by the home and community during that time.

The sad figures among the statistics of many churches are those which tell us that, of every two persons received on profession of faith, one drops out. Think of that the next time new members are taken into your church. Mentally cast half of them out the door again; simply because, many in leadership are succumbing to satanic influence and believe this is normal and to be expected.

Just as disastrous may be the unrecorded number of those who remain on church rolls, considered by themselves and others to be typical church members, but almost totally unaffected by the church and its faith. The whole impact of the church on the world is weakened because it has so many in its membership who have never really understood what the church is. On an average Sunday, I have observed that two-thirds of the members will not be at the churches to which they vowed to be loyal. One pastor noted, "Of every 100 enrolled members, 5 cannot be found, 20 never pray, 25 never read the Bible, 30 never attend a church, 40 never give to any cause, 50 never go to Sunday school, 60 never go to church at night, 70 never give to missions, 75 never do any church work, 80 never go to prayer meetings, 90 do not have family worship, 95 never win another soul to Christ."

We are so familiar with this record of failure that we are in danger of accepting it as something to be expected (it has become the new norm). God forbid! There is no law of nature or other reason to excuse it. It is the direct result of careless and unspiritual practices. This is shown by the fact those churches which give exceptional teaching and care to new members often keep more than 90 per cent of them. The casual way in which many churches leave it up to its new members to shift for themselves shows small regard for the solemn obligation it assumed in its expressed pledges of "koinonia love and nurture."

The church is an organism designed to enhance spiritual relationships. When authentic, biblical fellowship, koinonia, is missing, the church becomes a cold and empty place. But when koinonia is occurring, the church is a dynamic, pulsating environment in which people find themselves alive and blossoming in a godly spirituality.

Discipleship (Conversion and Conservation)

If we treated newborn babies as carelessly as we treat newborn Christians, the infant mortality rates would equal the appalling mortality of Church members. These "losses from the back door" are a major problem facing every denomination. The best place to prevent losses from the back door is proper love and reception at the front door.

Conversion and *conservation* are not competitors but companions, not opposites but likes. They join hands to lead the unsaved into the new birth and onward to the fullness of the stature of a man or woman of God in Christ. Conversion is the planting of the seed; conservation is the cultivating of that seed for a harvest. Conversion is the turning of an unsaved person from his or her evil ways to Christ; conservation is getting them started in the race; and helping them run the race with patience and persistence. The *purpose* of evangelism is to bring the unsaved to Christ, to make converts. The *goal* of evangelism is to make disciples and produce mature Christians.

The word disciple is used 230 times in the Gospels and 28 times in Acts. According to the New Testament usage of the word, a convert is a disciple [a learner]. The disciple is one who receives Jesus as his or her personal Savior, becomes a member in the church, the body of Christ, and commits to living under the reign of Jesus Christ in the way Jesus taught. At first the disciples may know very little. He or she may not know the full story of God's redeeming work from creation to re-creation. He or she may not know the full extent of what it means to submit to the lordship of Christ. The disciple may not know how to pray, how to read the Scriptures, how to live a godly spirituality (life). He or she may not know how to deal with evil, how to live in a countercultural way, or how to be an active member of the body of Christ. The disciple may not know what his or her gifts are or how to use them in the life of the church. He or she may not know how to see all of life as a Christian vocation.

Why is this? It's because the new disciple is an infant in the faith. He or she is now brought into the church, not as an adult with a mature perspective, but as an infant who needs to be nurtured and brought up in the faith. Just as we need to care for and nurture our offspring by bringing them into a healthy family where we love them, nurse them, and train them through the stages of life into maturity, so also the church is to do the same for the newly born spiritual infants. The new convert is a disciple just as much as the newborn baby is a human being. Most new disciples know almost nothing about the faith. They must be instructed and Spirit-formed.

For example, sometime ago while I was praying for some people at the altar a young visiting couple with two pre-school children and she was pregnant with a third came forward. I asked if they were Christians both answered that they were, I asked their names which they told me. I asked why they had different last names; he stated that they were not married. I had them to be seated until service was over. Later during our conversation I asked them about church membership. Though they had come to Christ two years earlier, and joined a church, they stated that no one had approached them concerning their lifestyle. They commented about other couples at their church living together then added, but no one talks about that at the church." That situation is not the exception today, but seems to be the rule in many churches as the "my rights" issue invades the church.

They had been cohabitating for four years. I told them that Christians lived together only after marriage. He told me that he thought that a marriage license was just another piece of paper and optional. He said, "Separation is out of the question though, because we have no place to go!" After further counsel, I prayed with them and a few days later they were married. They came back and joined the church seeking more truth of God's Word. That situation was resolved. Praise God! As secularism sets in, this will probably become a common occurrence; so we must be prepared to confront it.

Cultural Shift

Forms of godliness which deny the power of God makes it imperative that we pay special attention to convert conservation today. Fewer people are coming to the church with true Christian backgrounds, but those coming are fully exercised by the culture and society through public education, the media, and so-called cultural norms. An Islamic couple attended my weekly Bible class. Though they were American born, they only knew what they were taught in the Islamic religion. I have experienced the same with Jehovah Witnesses. Both of these religions put their converts through intense teaching and training. I personally taught and counseled these couples concerning Christianity and its requirements. I had them to attend the church for a while as our counseling sessions continued. Both couples had a hard time shaking what they had been taught about Jesus and the Holy Spirit. Eventually they stopped coming, returning to their former spirituality. With that said, I have several friends who converted from Islam to Christianity. They bring exuberance for soul-winning and care for the neighbor that is so vital to the church. It is so sad that for many American born citizens, Christianity is the foreign spirituality; we can thank multiculturalism and secularism for that. God forbid!

I was interim pastor of a cross-cultured congregation for 12 months in Korea. Though many of the younger Koreans came to learn and practice their English, it was amazing the truly Christian backgrounds they came from. I stress to pastors and teachers the importance of furthering their awareness through personal research and study, conferences, on-line information, or seeking some continuing education and training because it's very easy for your church to become a mixed multitude (with many different worldviews among their membership). We are in the Lord's army, and armies cannot survive without leaders and cadre personnel in specialized training capacities. Pastors get your leaders into training. Otherwise you will be overwhelmed by our ever changing multi-culture. The U.S. Military is very accommodating as for as religion is concerned; many religions are represented in its ranks. We seem to forget that cultures come with their own gods/religions. If we are not careful Christianity will be barred from our military forces, because it is not a religion. It is a life, and it is exclusive. Those who are insisting that it become inclusive are trying to make it just another religion [under the state!]. Religion adapts itself to the culture making it culturally driven. I noticed a sign on one of our military installations denoting a "high place." Do you remember "high places" in the Bible and God's attitude toward them?

Today, politically correct American leadership at all levels from the Executive branch of the government down to the town councils and school boards mock and turn their backs on the God of the Bible. Christians have at the same time allowed nonbelievers and the secularists to convince them that it's alright to place their God on the same level with the imported gods of other nations in violation of the first Commandment and a practice that runs counter to biblical warnings.

Take a few moments and read Deuteronomy 28:15-22 which clearly presents curses for willful disobedience. Is the cup of iniquity for this nation full? The same God whose virgin born Son Jesus Christ died for the sins of the world is very much alive. The same God whose Son went unchallenged as the only Way, the Truth, and the Life in this nation from its birth, until recently.

The biblical worldview makes clear, that our ultimate concern must be the glory of God. When Scripture instructs us to love God and to love our neighbor as ourselves, it gives us a mandate for the right kind of culture engagement. We love our neighbors; because we first love God. In His sovereign will God puts us within the cultural context in order to *display His glory by preaching the Gospel, confronting individuals with God's truth, and serving as salt and light in a dark and fallen world.* Therefore, the love of God within us leads us to love our neighbor, and to love our neighbor requires our participation in the culture and in the political process.

One thing that the cultural shift is causing in the church is forced change. In their search for a godly spirituality many [not just younger people] are entering the church and countering the status quo. While the status quo winks at sin to a certain extent for the sake of numbers, programs and church pride, these people want an authentic godly spirituality beginning with a separation from the world.

This morning on the news a church was praising God for hearing and answering their prayers miraculously. The church was in foreclosure due to the downturn in the economy. They believed God and an anonymous donor heard of their plight and paid the full amount of the mortgage some $300.000 plus dollars. If we would keep it real, you know Satan is not in the blessing business. So God should be glorified as He no doubt moved on this person's heart. The scripture says, "All good and perfect gifts come down from God the Father."

The current culture shift secularly is really a continuation of the sixties revolution in that it has taken on the nihilism of that particular period and concluded there is no universal explanation of life. In today's world, all ideas, all concepts, all systems of power, all ideologies, and all answers are suspect. The only thing you can count on is yourself—your ideas, your morality, and your goals. Born in academia this ungodly philosophy is now full-grown. God forbid!

I believe God's judgment is really about to come upon the House of God, but through His grace the Lord is allowing us some time to get it right. I tell my Bible students to stick with the truth of God's Word. Spirit-filled Christians grounded in the Word of God are being used mightily of God today in the marketplace for the kingdom of God. Today is the day for the saints to carry the gospel out of the four walls and into the streets [highways and hedges]. Remember, only the Word of God has the power to give life!

The Word of God draws! Reading the prior paragraph proves that the Bible is the only book today that really makes sense. In countries around the world where the people are now exposed to the truths of God's Word; conversions and miracles are taking place at a phenomenal rate; because they are grasping the truth at all cost, even death. While in this country where the Bible has been accessible from its beginning; America seems insistent in heading in the opposite direction.

In the early church, Christians took a strong anti-cultural stance. The same is expected of Christians today. We are called upon to live lives that are different. Christians are not to be shaped by ungodly spirituality (see Romans 6:12) or by the old Adamic nature (see Colossians 3:5-9), nor are they to walk according to the flesh, as if there is no God in heaven (see Galatians 5:19-21).

Instead the Christian life is shaped by being servants of righteousness (see Romans 6), by living according to the new humanity (Colossians 3:12-17), and walking after the Spirit (see Galatians 5:22-26). Converts must be taught that as they live in the structures of the world, in a counter cultural way they are Christ's transforming presence. The church becomes a transforming presence in the culture when Christians live by Christian virtues and values in the various structures of State—political, economic, institutional, educational, medical, etc. Christians make these structures function better by their presence within them and by the "salt and light" effect they have on people. Jesus motivates those who are His to live righteously by emphasizing that such living is the result of their new nature (see 2 Corinthians 5:17; John 3:3; Galatians 5:22-25).

The home remains God's first and greatest institution. God established the home before He established the church, or the state for the welfare and blessing of His human family. As great as the emphasis is placed on the family in Christian homes, the fact is many Christian homes are not the happy, Spirit-led homes as defined in the Scriptures. Never were there more perils which threaten our home life today, and never was a true, strong, spiritual home life needed more than now. What are some of these dangers that threaten our homes?

The list is a long and discouraging one, including divorce, cohabitation, irreverent children, the breakdown of parental authority, abuses, extravagant spending, making the home just a place to eat and sleep, wrong purposes and motives, selfishness on the part of parents and children, lack of prayer and Bible reading and family worship in the home. It is not enough for parents and children to go to Sunday school together. If we would make our homes truly Christian we must realize that Christianity is a life, not just a matter of nominal church membership.

The importance of the home is huge from the standpoint of the fruits that it produces in personal character and style of life. One of the dangers that Christian parents face today is that of passing our spiritual responsibility for our children over to somebody else. The church down the street can help us, but the church that is in our homes is the institution to which we must first look, and as we are responsible for the functioning of that church, Christian parents must accept the challenge of teaching the next generation according to (Deuteronomy 6:6-8). When this mandate to train children in the truth of God's word is carried out their ability to live counter to the culture is solidified enabling them to hold on to their faith. These young people are equipped to defend their faith in high school, college and life when faced with contrary belief systems and non-biblical world views.

The Book of Proverbs could be called the Biblical Manual for Training Children. For example, let's look at a passage misquoted and overlooked by the home and the church. That is, *"Train up a child in the way that he [she] should go, and when he [she] is old he [she] will not depart from it" (see Proverbs 22:6)*. Brackets are mine. This Proverb is a very important message from our Lord to Christian parents; it consists of a command and a promise:

- Train up a child in the way that he [she] should go. That is a command: Meaning bring up the child in the admonition [Word] of the Lord (especially during the formative years ages 1-12).

- Leading the child to Christ at the earliest opportunity is imperative.

- Provide a consistent example in the home.

The promise follows:

When he is old he [or she] will not depart from it. Notice this passage promises that the child *will not* depart. Many interpret it to say "if they depart; they will return." That's not what it says. In our earthy thinking "to not depart" seems so impossible in our own strength and it is. However, if we consider this is a promise in the Word of God; which means if we do our part, God will do His and keep our children, so they will not depart.

We find the prime example in Paul's writing to Timothy emphasizing the young minister's godly heritage. He bases his confidence in him on the fact that from a child he has known the Holy Scriptures, which are able to make wise unto salvation through faith in Jesus Christ (see 2 Timothy 3:15). Someone asked a wise teacher how early he thought the Christian training of a child should begin. He answered quickly, "With its grandmother!" Why? Note the three generations [grandmother, mother, and Timothy]. The child must repent and believe for themselves, but it would be impossible to overestimate the advantage of a child who has been reared in a Christian atmosphere and who has been led toward Christ from the first moment of his or her life. We live our lives empowered by the Holy Spirit and the Word of God.

Another truth is, if we would rear a generation of Christian workers to take our places, the men and women of the future would carry on the work of the churches and extend the limits of the kingdom of God. We must, produce them in the soil of a Christian atmosphere. A convert is a disciple. Whatever Jesus calls disciples to do, they do. The issue is not "now that you are a convert, I suggest you consider being a disciple." The making of a new disciple is the work of the church. Most local churches admit they are having successes in receiving converts, but I'm sure that most will agree that a *desperate need* exists for a process that takes the new disciple by the hand and leads him or her toward maturity.

There is hope! The emerging generation of leaders grew up inside the culture of the late twentieth century. Many of these young emerging leaders in the church show much promise; as they came up during the rise of this secular, post-Christian "everything goes" and "no absolutes" culture of relativism; which is futile to those who are seeking and receiving the truth of God's Word. For this reason the emerging church is more countercultural than the traditional church. This church calls for an honest, authentic faith that seeks to be the church. They are shaking off the shackles of denominationalism, customs and traditions of men, and seeing the church through new eyes. Christ has touched their hearts for those who are lost.

The Doctrine

The misunderstanding of what happens when a person joins the church has caused a great deal of the unrealistic practices in the local churches. We assumed that a profession of faith in Christ equated to a soul being born into the kingdom and regeneration having taken place. In America what comprise Christianity to many is dependent upon who is talking or holding certain positions. The DJ playing Christmas carols could give his or her rendition hitting several emotional notes and people would believe that according to their talent they are Christian. In some cases it boils down to one person asking another, "Would you like to be a Christian?" If he or she answers in the affirmative they are told something like, "Come to our church Wednesday night and during mid-week services the pastor will make you one." God forbid!

Requirements for church membership seems to be held lightly or non existent because of the numbers game, facility size and other non-biblical man-made standards. Today in many local churches coming forward at altar call equates to a salvation experience. No testimony or statement of faith required. 2 Peter 1:5 indicates that because of all of the God-given blessings in vv. 3, 4 there is something beyond the new birth; and that is spiritual growth. This demands diligence and earnestness; not indifference or self-satisfaction. Biblically speaking the church properly launches her born again converts into the Christian life only as she *fully* obeys the tenets of the Great Commission, Matthew 28:19-20:

> *"Go therefore and make disciples of all the nations,*
> ***baptizing them** in the name of the Father and of the*
> *Son and of the Holy Spirit, **teaching them** to observe*
> *all things that I have commanded you; and lo, I am*
> *with you always even to the end of the age."*

The kind of evangelism called for in this commission does not end with the conversion of the unbeliever. The Great Commission puts "baptizing" before "teaching them to observe all things"—which is the part we are too likely to neglect. The three thousand who were baptized on the Day of Pentecost immediately went into *intensive care ["teaching"]*.

The statement *"the Lord added to their number day by day those who were being saved"* indicates that more time and nurture is required within the church (see Acts 2:42 and 47). The situation that I have been expounding on is seen in Acts 8:14-17, as the Samaritans progressed toward being full Christians they stopped just after they had been baptized—very similar to what happens in too many churches in this country today!

When we lead the new members to believe that salvation is finished when he or she joins the church, it's no wonder that they think they are doing all that is necessary so like the beaming old graduates, they return for the annual reunion each Easter Sunday.

The Historical Aspect

The Church born on the Day of Pentecost did not require much preparation since they were all first generation Christians and beginners. In fact the whole church was made up of new members. A check of church history revealed that the centuries immediately following, however, required beginners to wait for a two to three year probation period before they were fully admitted to the community of established Christians. They were given:

- Intensive training.
- Examined for evidences of genuine faith.

These early church practices were established in some foreign lands by western missionaries and remain in place to this day; though sad to say many sponsoring nations have long since abandoned them. One practice in many Korean churches is that the candidate has to bring another person to Christ before they can be received into the church. During our tour in Korea my wife and I became acquainted with two World records in the Christian church:

- The world's largest church is Yoido Full Gospel Pentecostal Church, Pastor Dr. Paul Y. Cho located in Seoul, Korea. The membership was at 200, 000 members when we were there 1980-82. Today it has over 1 million members. 171 assistant pastors and 356 lay pastors. The church is listed in the Guinness Book of World records.

- Korea sends out many foreign missionaries, it has been reported to be more than any other nation.

In America too many local churches will receive anyone who will express a desire and accept a brief statement of faith. Up until 60 or so years ago, this practice was widespread in the local churches for various reasons. Just to name a few:

- The culture was at least nominally Christian.
- The Judea-Christian worldview was widely accepted by saints and sinners.
- It was difficult to assume that those outside the church were not in a sense Christian.
- Their rational was that the miracle of regeneration was more likely to happen within the fellowship than out in the cold on probation.
- Some believed that any hindrance with the impulse to join the church was an interference with the working of the Holy Spirit.

Many of the liturgical Churches prescribe confirmation classes for both children and adults, while many Pentecostal/ Charismatic Churches seek evidence that the Holy Spirit has been received. Today the tendency seems to be to snatch anyone into the church at the first evidence that they are willing to come in. Trying to make admission to the local churches so easy and painless has drawn many into church membership without a true conversion experience. Many of these are there for what they can get out of it; and once that ceases to happen they move on.

Even after the church has done all she can do; many converts fail to reach maturity and desert both Christ and His church. Judas left his Lord with the voice of Jesus ringing in his ears and the impression of the Last Supper imprinted on his mind. Paul watched his fellow helper, Demas walk away from his holy purpose and gave the explanation of his departure: *"Demas hath forsaken me, having loved this present world" (see 2 Timothy 4:10).*

Many times neither the church nor their pastor is to blame when a convert fails. A new convert or an old Christian always retains the power of personal choice. The final battle for Christian maturity is fought between the convert's two ears [as the battle rages in their mind], in spiritual warfare.

Spiritual Warfare

There are many people in the churches today who are held hostage in their minds by the devil. In order to free these people from this demonic oppression; disciples must know how to recognize the work of the enemy; and how to overcome his attacks against the mind. Satan's goal is to plant a stronghold of deception in some area of an individual's mind. If he is successful, he can control and manipulate the person from that lofty position.

The Holy Spirit is obviously speaking very strongly to the churches today concerning spiritual warfare. Christian leaders and churches all across this nation are awakening to this reality. In light of this, we must give heed to what the Spirit is saying to the churches and proceed with the Holy Spirit and the Word of God as our guide and foundation.

As we engage in spiritual warfare, we must realize that this level of maturing involves more than just dealing with the devil. Other major elements are the renewing of our minds and crucifying the flesh. The truth is, the devil's attacks against our lives will not work if our flesh does not cooperate. When we truly mortify the flesh (see Colossians 3:5), living lives that are "dead to sin" (see Romans 6:2) as we are commanded to do in Scripture, we will not respond to demonic suggestions and fleshly temptation. Dead men and women are incapable of responding to anything. Therefore, we see the power of a crucified life.

The above declaration will not work if that person has willfully permitted some area of the mind to go unchecked and unguarded. Additionally, if he or she is aware of an area of sin that has not been dealt with it opens the door for Satanic attack. In that case his or her prayers against the devil will not avail because the real enemy here is their own carnal mind and flesh; which must be submitted to the control of the Holy Spirit in order to eradicate these attacks.

If people focus only on Satan as they pursue the subject of spiritual warfare and fail to consider other equally important areas, this emphasis will be very damaging to them. We must be careful to remember that the real battle with Satan was won at the Cross and the Resurrection. Now this same victorious Christ who single-handedly defeated Satan lives in us in the Person of the Holy Spirit. That is why the beloved apostle John admonishes us, "Greater is He that is in you, than he that is in the world" (1 John 4:4).

The Practical Requirements

New converts/ members require much which they will not get in the average program of the church for all its members. Pastors who believe that their sermons will serve as the Communicants' instructions are not very realistic:

- New members have a tremendous amount of catching up to do which must be done in a direct and intensive way. They also have access baggage to unload from earlier life experiences.
- They do not have the feel, the knowledge, or the attitude which healthy church participation requires.
- Without special attention they are likely to assume that their immature state is actually the norm for church members. This is especially true for those of age. When they come to Christ, we should treat them with dignity and at the same time feed them [as the babes they are] with the milk of the Word.
- The shifting of the population has many converts on the move due to jobs and other opportunities before being fully developed; and in many cases they may never grow up.

It is imperative that converts be taught and Spirit-formed while they are still teachable. Experience reflects that after people have been in the church about a year, they are likely to assume that their opinions on religious matters are as good as anyone's.

- From then on trying to change them, very much may seem to the presumptuous.
- It is during the period of joining that people are most humbly ready to be taught and shown what church members ought to be.
- New members may not understand that Christians are a different kind of being, with a completely *different* way of thinking, living, and dying. *"If any man be in Christ, he is a new creature"* *(II Corinthians 5:17).*
- People may think of joining the church simply as a helpful connection, instead of as entering into a new and *all-inclusive* way of life.
- The church may be embraced by those whose opinions and decisions are shaped entirely by the motives of the world.
- Those who have formed outside the church their business ethics, their attitudes toward other races, and their ways of having a good time, along with their ideas on the use of money are likely to retain them without change unless they are shown the peculiarly biblical worldview of such areas.
- New habits are very hard for adults to start or stop. New members will need help and guidance if there is to be a change in their long established worldview, customs of speech, habit of home life.
- Regular participation in the Sunday services is very important in bringing new members into Christian fellowship and understanding.
- When people are told to read their Bibles without being told how, they are likely to get bogged down.
- Exhortations to pray without practical instructions may prove futile.
- Many church members have remained passive in public worship because they have never understood just what is expected of the worshipper.

- Every church that's bringing real godly spirituality into the lives of people is giving its converts and new members, meticulous instructions and applicable opportunities.
- We must preach and teach the gospel of Christ until the unsaved ones believes and are converted.
- We must continue to teach and preach the gospel of Christ so that the new converts will grow into maturity [discipleship].
- This is the Master's plan for evangelism. The church today must not do less!
- We must never forget that the Christian is saved to serve. In the unselfish service of others he or she is most like their Master, and through this unselfish service the door is open is for Christ to come into many hearts.
- We must always be on the look out for opportunities to help those in need, to minister to those who are sick, to comfort those who are in sorrow, and to do kindness to those whom we meet every day, then we will never be without opportunity to witness for Christ.
- Is it not strange that so many of us should have forgotten this ideal to which we committed ourselves when we accepted Christ? We need not expect our witness to be with power unless it is backed up by lives of unselfish service.

Peter's Checklist

In II Peter 1:5-7, the words, ***"But also for this very reason,"*** (v. 5) indicates that there is something beyond the new birth. There is growth! It's not enough to be born into God's family, we must also grow spiritually. This demands diligence and earnestness. A lazy, careless, Christian does not grow. The apostle Peter lists the spiritual characteristics that ought to be seen in each disciple's life. He is not suggesting that we add these virtues like we add beads to a string necklace. Rather, each characteristic helps us develop the next one. This biblical checklist lays out for us what must be covered in the training, assimilation and growth of new converts to maturity:

(1) **Faith**—to faith we add virtue (love for Christ—dedication of life to Him).

(2) **Virtue**—to virtue we add knowledge (moral discernment; Christians must be able to discern right from wrong and have a biblical worldview.).

(3) **Knowledge**—to knowledge we add self-control (patience and endurance. Christians must have "staying power" in times of trials.

(4) **Self-control**—to self-control we add steadfastness (strength of character).

(5) **Steadfastness**—to steadfastness we add godliness (see v. 3). This word means "right worship" or dependence on God that reveals itself in a devoted life.

(6) **Godliness**—to godliness we add brotherly love (meaning a love for the people of God).

(7) **Brotherly love**—to brotherly love [phileo] we add koinania [agape] the "as Christ loved us," love for one another.

(8) **Koinania** (agape, the final virtue Peter names is charity, old English (for love which "wraps"), all the virtues together into one.

These spiritual characteristics of teaching and training should be incorporated and considered for new converts. Those who are received by letters of transfer also require special care:

- The new congregation will not seem like the familiar friends back home.
- The new way of doing things may seem wrong.
- Homesickness may turn into resentment for the new church.
- Adjustment to a new place may crowd out church habits.

It is therefore important that those who come by transfer be brought into as much of the new member training as possible. This process for all converts and transfers begins with a conference with the pastor. While it might not seem realistic to require loyal, long-time members from another church to attend classes on belief and churchmanship, they are probably anxious to attend. They will need the introduction to the various organizations of the church. All the ways of making them feel a part of the church family are particularly important—calls, social events, and small group.

Regardless of how high tech our evangelism training or how highly specialized our programs, the church must always hold before itself the ultimate goals and growth standards for new converts as outlined in God's Word, ". . . . *till we all come in the unity of the faith and of the knowledge of the Son of God, unto a perfect man, unto the measure of the stature of the fullness of Christ" (Ephesians 4:13)*.

Organizing for New Members Conservation

Abuse of congregational freedom [stemming from so-called individual rights] is at an all-time high today and responsible for the inadequate care of new members. Most local churches do very little for them beyond the pastor's sermon and the welcome to the fellowship handshake from the congregation. I will say from experience this responsibility cannot be left to the pastor alone. Christians do not save themselves or keep themselves saved—but it is the Christian's responsibility to know without a doubt that he or she is saved (Read I Thessalonians 1:5-10), and possesses the marks of a believer. The Apostle Paul points out these marks in the people of the church of Thessalonica. They distinguished these Christians and Christians today should bear these same marks (evidences) of salvation in their lives. Notice in 1 Thessalonians 1:4-5:

- **Work of Faith**—When people truly trust Christ, their faith will be shown by works. Works will not save, but faith that does not lead to works is not saving faith. True Christian faith results in a changed life (see James 2:14-26).
- **Labor of love**—an unsaved individual lives for his or herself (see Ephesians 2:1-2), but the true born-again Christian is willing to work because of love. He or she has a new motivation for living; and that is they love Christ and others (see Hebrews 10:24-25).
- **Patience in hope**—The lost are without hope. The true Christians have endurance in the trials of life because they know Christ is coming again. They don't give up because they know He is coming to deliver them (see 1 Peter 1:1-9; 4:12-16). Faith, hope, and love are marks (evidences) of true salvation (see Colossians 1:4-5; Romans 5:1-4).

Many churches attempt to operate and reach people in today's anti-Christian culture with methods that worked with people in *yesterday's* churched culture. Most of their soul-winning and conservation methods are left over from the pre and post World War II generations. The thinking is that if they worked back then, they should still work today and they will still work tomorrow. This would certainly be true—*if our culture never changed*. But it does change, and these churches must pray and think through how this cultural change affects their conversion and conservation methods. Think through the following examples:

- Bumper stickers with the words "Jesus Saves," the "sign of the fish," "large crosses" on chains around the neck or dangling from ear lobes, and the like are a turn off for most unsaved people. They think this is weird and fits their lifestyles.
- Other than Christians, who listens to Christian radio and watches Christian television?

- City-wide evangelistic crusades have turned into another method for church fellowship, because they are not attracting the unsaved.

- The confrontational approach which had its higher success in the 60's and 70's only comprise of about 5-10% of the churches membership. Why? Only about that percentage of members have the gift of evangelism and are comfortable with a confrontational approach.

- Up until the late 50's and 60's America was predominately a churched culture. Even in the early 80's the church had some influence. I was pastor of a church in a county where we had and agreement with the school system. They scheduled nothing on Wednesday nights and we scheduled nothing at church on Friday nights. I was there for six years and this church, community, and school relationship was a beauty to behold. Why don't we have this type of community connection [with young people] today?

The Judeo-Christian influence was strong on most institutions and organizations, including public school systems, national, state, local governments; and the business sector. As the result of a number of decisions by the Supreme Court, this is no longer the case. In fact many of these organizations are prohibited by law from displaying any Christian symbols or sponsoring public prayer or Bible reading. All of this has affected the typical post modern person in this country. While some are hostile, many look on Christianity as simply irrelevant to them and the times. As a result they have adopted a thoroughly secular mind-set and listing themselves as atheists [a person who does not believe in God].

There are those in the local church who remember the old days and what church was like; they enjoy reminiscing [and in so many words living in the past]. At the same time, the only knowledge their children have of Christianity is extracted from what they see on television or in the movies. We may live in the same neighborhoods, in some cases the same home, cheer for the same teams, and even speak the same language, *but our core values are worlds apart!*

The mentality of most people in society today is focused on the present not the future. They don't think about eternity because that is not important to them. These people can't deal with such phrases and words such as *"wait a while," "patience,"* or *"commitment,"* they are not in their vocabulary. A 90's slogan for Burger King advertised, "Have it your way!" People want everything and they want it now. The results of such a philosophy of life shows the extreme frustrations, high amount of deep emotional scars, suicides, and divorce rates. This generation keeps the appointment schedules of psychologists, and psychiatrists booked solid.

To reach people today, the churches will have to show the benefits of Christianity in the present day. It will have to demonstrate in life and teaching that Christianity addresses the hard issues of life, such as who are we, where we came from, what are we worth, why are we here, and where are we going? A through biblically-based worldview would fill this need. I recently read an article wherein a minister and a palm reader had a conversation. The minister asked, "Why did you become a palm reader?" He answered, "I was a Christian and spent a lot of time at a revival searching for the power of God. When I couldn't seem to find it, I started dabbling in the occult and even voodoo," then he added: "All that scared me, and I decided to study palm reading because it seemed safer." Then he said, "Now, tell me why you do what you do" (referring to his being a minister). He stated, "I preach the gospel and for two primary reasons:

- First, the gospel is the only thing on the planet that can tell a person what is really wrong with them. You see the gospel tells us that the source of *our* pain is separation from God because of sin. As we have broken God's moral laws it has resulted in our lives and our souls becoming broken."
- The man was genuinely listening. He went on, "The second reason I preach the gospel, Is because it's the only

thing on this planet that can tell us what to do to heal our condition." He then stated the gospel clearly and offered him God's answer for his life. The man thanked him and actually allowed him to pray for him. The seed of the gospel was planted that one day may bear fruit.

Today is the day of the saints; and many are being activated and enabled to share their faith using this definition of the gospel: *"The gospel is the good news that God became man in Jesus Christ. He lived the life that we should have lived and died the death we should have died—in our place. Three days later He rose from the dead, proving He is the Son of God and offering the gift of salvation to everyone who repents and believes the gospel."* We no longer can be content just to bring people to the church where the pastor will preach the gospel. We must see the millions of true Christians in America equipped and empowered to share the gospel of Christ as they [go among them].

The church should adapt its *practices*, **not in its faith**; to the people it's trying to reach. (Another word used for adaptation is *contextualization.)* These *practices* concern cultural things (the world in here)—when the church meets, which translation of the Bible it uses, the instruments used in worship, casual versus formal dress, and so on. Paul teaches this principle in 1 Corinthians 9:19-23 and 10:23-33. It's also demonstrated by Jesus' ministry (see, for example, John 3-4). In practicing cultural and individual adaptation, the church **must never compromise in any way the clear teaching of Scripture.** We cannot expect lost people to come to us on our terms and adjust to the church's unique culture. That simply will not happen! The *mature* church must be willing to be flexible and put aside its own cultural and individual preferences [and hang-ups] to reach the lost. For example:

- Will we take off our coat and tie or over look the lack of our traditional church dress code; if lost people will come to our meeting?

- If they will come only at 10:00 AM, will we design a special service for them and meet as believers at another time?
- If they prefer to park up close to the front are we willing to park further away and walk?
- What are we willing to give up in order to reach the lost? The Father was willing to give up His Son (see John 3:16). The Son was willing to give up His life (see Romans 5:8). Paul was willing to give up his soul (see Romans 9:3). In light of this, we must ask, what are we willing to give up?

A group of spiritually mature Christians should be commissioned in every church to intercede for new converts. New member conservation training is the other *half* of evangelism and therefore requires the whole church's involvement. The officers must never have a chance to forget the overall command is to "make disciples."

- Teaching the leadership basic principles of discipleship is the first step in preparing the whole church for building a solid on-going ministry of follow-up.
- A closely related objective is to train among the leaders a team of disciplers skilled in dealing individually with new believers.
- By developing a discipleship team trained for individual attention and congregational attention through small groups; then the church can lead new converts into a consistent godly lifestyle.

The convert now must be taught and enabled to learn by application to live a productive godly life. Prior to our spiritual nature being resurrected from the death of sin; we were burdened with a sinful ungodly spirituality inherited from our natural nature. Now in possession of life in Christ, the new convert is ready to move on to maturity in discipleship.

Small Group Ministry

Many churches across this nation are setting records of growth, evangelism, and Spiritual-formation. One of the common threads through all of these churches is an advanced small group structure. I am an advocate of this ministry methodology, having used it in my later pastoral experiences and now as a foundational tool in church planting. Many churches are striving to survive on the weekly Bible study, with about 5% of the membership. Asked why the attendance is so poor:

- People say they are too busy to attend another meeting.
- They don't want to get bogged down with participating in programs, events, and meetings.
- As stated in an earlier chapter. Bible studies without "action-living mission" dies.
- Small groups are more than curriculum, charts, organizational manuals and a vision statement.
- Merely changing the name from committee or department to small group ministry is not enough. Each group must see in its purpose authentic relationships that builds and empowers the whole person in community, (the body of Christ) to in turn impacts the world.

Small groups help churches organize the scattered members of the church and make them into a body with "tendons, flesh and skin." These small groups are to be more than people connected by an organizational structure. It's like Ezekiel's vision of the dry bones (see Ezekiel 37:1-14). We can contrast what he saw with the average small group endeavor. He saw the bones connected and covered with new flesh and he said, *"There was no breath in them."* It wasn't enough for the bones to be joined properly. Without the breath of God, the bodies were still dead. But when the breath entered them, *"they came to life and stood on their feet—a vast army."*

In order for the church to operate according to God's design, it isn't enough for the people to be connected in small groups. These groups must have the breath of God flowing through them to work. We will list a few aspects of the breath of God moving through the group:

- The small group's focus is the kingdom mission. Mark tells us that Jesus came announcing the "Good News" of the kingdom of God. The strategy in the small group meeting is to allow the good news of the kingdom to transform our lives as we share together. God is calling His people to a new way of living that is oriented around His reign and relationship.

- God is love. At the center of God's essence is love, which means He prioritizes relationships over all else (see John 13:34). So the small group is a place where people have deep, abiding relationships with Jesus Christ and with one another. Small groups grow and multiply. That's a documented fact. But they do so because the people in them have learned to love one another, not because of some program that has been perfectly designed for them. Churches must high light love and cultivate an atmosphere where people have time to love one another and not be bogged down with participating in programs, events, and meetings. The following verses provides a wonderful sample for a small group lesson:

Love never gives up.
Love cares more for others than for self.
Love doesn't want what it doesn't have.
Love doesn't strut, doesn't have a swelled head,
Doesn't force itself on others,
Isn't always "me first,"
Doesn't fly off the handle, doesn't keep score

On the sins of others,
Doesn't revel when others grovel,
Takes pleasure in the flowing of truth,
Puts up with anything,
Trusts God always, always looks for the best,
Never looks back, but keeps going to the end.
Love never dies.
1 Corinthians 13:4-8, The Message

The counsel in this passage contains some of the things my wife and I do personally in our home and with our children, grandchildren, and great grandchildren to protect our marriage and family. This is not only a great lesson for small group, but you can use this as a checklist and to see how many things you can check off as things you also practice. On those things you are having problems with and therefore can't check off, consider trying one of them each week, and then observe the results.

- What takes place in the small group meeting? What curriculum should we use? God doesn't want us to focus upon man's formulas. He never intended for us to depend upon man's curriculum or methods in our ministry to one another. They should only be a vehicle in which we experience God's presence. Jesus said, *"Where two or three are gathered together in My name, there I am also."* A small group meeting without Christ's presence has been compared to a golfing class where the students study the plays but never get to play the game." The group does more than study and talk about Jesus; they make room for Him to show up and touch people's lives.
- The experience of the presence of God in corporate worship feeds the experience of Christ in small groups. Small groups work with the large group in worship services; they don't replace them. Nor will small group members know how to recognize the presence of Christ in small group without knowing God's presence in the large

group worship. Churches that experience the presence of God corporately are much more likely to develop groups that work.

- The pastor must work with key leaders to develop one vision around which the whole church can unify. This combats the problem of multi-visions. Then he or she must lead the people into the overall vision of which relationships is the key and be committed to making sure the unified vision is established.

- Small group members have the potential to be positive influences in the group to the extent they are walking in spiritual freedom from sin. The problem is that sin is often hidden and people are controlled by condemnation. Or the sin of their past still controls them. Freedom and spiritual victory are brought to many in small group due to intentional strategy to lead people into the experience of spiritual victory.

- The small groups aren't new in the church. But traditional groups usually have a singular purpose. Small groups should be wholistic; and they shouldn't divide up the Christian life into parts and ask people to only do that one part. Wholistic groups accomplish both the Great Commandment and the Great Commission. When the Spirit of God is alive in the group, He moves through the people to love God and one another, while also reaching out to the unsaved. While no two wholistic groups will be the same because they'll reach different kinds of people, all wholistic groups have the same purpose: the Great Commandment and the Great Commission. Likewise, you may experience different types of groups (fishing groups, book groups, coffee break groups—just to name a few), but they still should be wholistic and Christ-centered in their spiritual purpose.

- The small group strategy is also a leadership strategy. A church won't have anymore groups than leaders, no matter how many people want to join them. Jesus instructed us to pray that the Lord of the harvest would send workers. The problem isn't a lack of harvest—it's ripe! The problem is that there aren't enough leaders to work the harvest. Tomorrow's leaders are today's small group members; many may not look like they have the potential to lead a group, but members won't become leaders by the snap of a finger. The churches that are the best at developing leaders have established a clear discipleship path that will help people walk in a godly spirituality, and then into leadership. Does each small group leader have an apprentice? If not—why not?

- When a church embraces this kind of wholistic ministering structure above, the heat of spiritual warfare will increase. Satan, the enemy of our souls doesn't want the church to experience this kind of godly spirituality. We know that he will try to create fear and weariness, but the small groups that work don't focus on what he is doing. Instead they concern themselves with becoming the army that Ezekiel saw in his vision, people mobilized to fight the spiritual battle, to take back what has been taken.

- We often read, "If every true church of Jesus Christ in the world should enlist all its truly saved members in the supreme business of finding and winning others, beginning where they are and extending their witness unto the uttermost part of the earth, the gospel message could be brought with the power of the Holy Spirit to nearly every soul in the world within this generation!"

They enter this battle by interceding for those who can't pray for themselves. They pray for the impossible, seeking God to work miracles in the lives of fellow small group members and unsaved friends. As they pray, they expect God to move through them in spiritual gifts, truly acting as the body of Christ. Take a look at each of the points above, and determine where your church is in the process, and ask God to breathe on the small group ministry in your church.

REFLECTION

*"My son, give me your heart and let your
eyes observe and delight in my ways."
(Proverbs 23:26 Amplified Bible).*

Study Responses (Chapter 18)

1. The most important thing I learned from this chapter was:

2. The area that I need to work on the most is:

3. I can apply this lesson to my life by:

4. Closing statement of Commitment:

A FINAL WORD

LIVING A GODLY SPIRITUALITY

*"But seek first the kingdom of God and His
righteousness, and all these things shall be added to you
(Matthew 6:33).*

Christ points to God's care of nature—the flowers, grass, and birds. "You are of more value than they. Certainly God will care for you!" The Father knows our needs, and if we put Him first, He will meet every need. How do believers today practice Matthew 6:33? In our previous state the grip of spiritual death gave us a mind-set to sin, an ungodly spirituality.

Now Christ begins imparting new godly spirituality [life in Christ] by transforming our thoughts, actions, feelings, and ambitions so they conform to Him through a new nature. The Bible contains all the revelation needed to learn to live the new life in the Spirit. We will start with our time, and put God first in every day. This means setting time for prayer, reading and studying the Word of God. We will put God first in every week, attending God's house faithfully. We will put God first every payday, paying the tithe to the Lord. We will put God first in our choices, making no decision that would leave God out.

There are spiritual parallels for the material things people seek today. We should seek to feed the hidden person of the heart with spiritual food just as we seek to feed the body physical food (see Matthew 4:4; 1 Peter 3:4). We should see that our spiritual garments are in order (Colossians 3:7-12) just as we fret over the physical garments that clothe our body. We drink physical water, but we should also drink the spiritual water of life that Christ offers (John 4:13-14; 7:37-39). In James 1:14 we read, *But each one is tempted when he [or she] is **drawn away** by his [or her] own desires and enticed.* This verse expresses the intensity of this present day in which desire lures an individual until he or she is tragically entrapped. Sin does not force itself on the unwilling, but **is chosen** because of its attractions. "Let us live godly lives, *so that we will not be drawn away.*"

Difficulties are to be expected in the Christian's life. The Scripture teaches that those who live godly should expect persecution (see 2 Timothy 3:12). In fact, Christ warned His disciples, that they would experience the same type of rejection He had experienced (see John 15:18-21). Satan has turned up the heat of persecution and rejection worldwide today knowing he has but a short time. However, you are encouraged to continue living a godly life in Christ. And *rejoice* that you have been considered worthy of sharing in Christ's suffering! In 1 Thessalonians 3:8, Paul encourages, ***"For now we live, if you stand fast in the Lord."*** The godly spirituality (life) is not governed by a set of rules. A few simple fundamental principles will suffice for your guidance in countering the ungodly spirituality:

- Turn from sin believe and receive the gospel; and trust Christ as your personal Savior.
- Confess Christ openly, in baptism and faithful church membership.
- Stay close to Christ through daily prayer and the study of His Word, through worship, and fellowship with His people.

- Live a clean, upright life, in accordance with the Sermon on the Mount and the Golden Rule.
- Be a good and faithful steward of time, gifts, influence, and possessions.
- Serve the Lord with gladness and win others to love and serve the Savior.

When we became Christians we committed ourselves to the ideal of obedience. "How true have we been to it?" Jesus has the final word of challenge with the question, *"Why call ye me Lord, Lord, and do not the things which I say?" (Luke 6:46 KJV)*

And I heard, as it were, the voice of a great
multitude, as the sound of many waters and as the
sound of mighty thundering, saying, "Alleluia!"
For the Lord God Omnipotent reigns!
Let us be glad and rejoice and give Him
glory, for the marriage of the Lamb has come,
and His wife has made herself ready."
And to her it was granted to be arrayed
in fine linen, clean and bright, for the fine
linen is the righteous acts of the saints.
(Revelation 19:6).